Decline of the Dollar

A Marxist View of the Monetary Crisis

Ernest Mandel

MONAD PRESS, NEW YORK

DISTRIBUTED BY
PATHFINDER PRESS, INC., NEW YORK

"The International Monetary Crisis" is Chapter Eight of *Europe vs. America* by Ernest Mandel, copyright © 1970 by New Left Books; reprinted by permission of Monthly Review Press. "The Crisis of the International Monetary System" is reprinted with permission from the March-April 1969 issue of the *International Socialist Review*. "Wilson's Quid Pro Quo With World Imperialism," "De Gaulle Doesn't Know It But the Golden Days of Capitalism are Over," "The Pound Sterling Bows Out as the Queen of Moneys," "The Dollar Crisis I," and "The Dollar Crisis II" are reprinted with permission from the December 4, 1964; February 19, 1965; December 8, 1967; January 19, 1968; and April 12, 1968 issues of *World Outlook* respectively. Other articles previously published are reprinted with permission from *Intercontinental Press* as follows: "The Crisis of the French Franc," December 9, 1968; "The Devaluation of the French Franc," September 8, 1969; "Revaluation of the Deutsche Mark," October 27, 1969; "The Open Decline of the Dollar," May 24, 1971; "The Deepening Crisis of the Imperialist System," September 6, 1971; "The Downfall of the Dollar," September 6, 1971; and "The Monetary Crisis Continues," January 10, 1972; copyright © 1968, © 1969, and © 1971 by *Intercontinental Press*.

Published by Monad Press
for the Anchor Foundation, Inc.

Distributed by
Pathfinder Press, Inc.
410 West Street
New York, N.Y. 10014

Library of Congress Catalog Card No. 72-85799
Manufactured in the United States of America

Contents

Part II

Introduction

In the resort village of Bretton Woods, New Hampshire, in the autumn of 1944, representatives of forty-four governments ratified an American plan for a new international monetary system to be built around a dollar that was "as good as gold."

According to this scheme, the dollar would be redeemable in gold at $35 an ounce and all other currencies would be pegged to the dollar at fixed exchange rates. The dollar, being solidly backed by gold, could then serve as a "reserve currency," which along with gold could be used by any country to settle international debts arising from current economic transactions. The British pound was designated as a secondary reserve currency, to be backed by dollars. The central role assigned to the dollar accorded with the predominant position of the United States in world trade and finance at the end of the second world war and the fact that the U. S. held most of the world's gold reserves.

An additional feature of this new monetary arrangement was the International Monetary Fund (IMF). This agency, headquartered in Washington, was to hold a pool of currencies and gold paid in by member governments, out of which short-term credit could be extended to countries experiencing temporary balance of payments deficits.

The monetary system launched at Bretton Woods fulfilled the hopes of its sponsors for little more than a decade. The first signs of serious trouble appeared after the 1957-58 U. S. recession, the third and deepest of the post-World War II downturns. Between 1957 and 1960, the United States ran a balance of payments deficit totaling over $10 billion. The resulting gold drain reduced the U. S. gold stock by more than $5 billion, bringing it down for the first time to a level that failed to cover the total of dollars held abroad. [1]

Why is it that the monetary system devised at Bretton Woods and the dollar it was built around went into decline? And in the midst of the most sustained economic expansion the United States, Western Europe, and Japan had ever experienced? And why have the governments of these countries been

5

unable to reverse the dollar's decline and overcome the monetary crisis despite many cooperative efforts to do so? These are among the questions Ernest Mandel takes up in this collection of articles written between 1964 and 1971.

Mandel's analysis flows from his view that monetary crises merely express much more deep-seated contradictions of modern capitalism. Foremost among these is the gap between society's productive capacity and the buying power of the workers, a gap that tends to widen as capitalist competition intensifies. Mandel argues that under capitalism the state is compelled to intervene in the economy, particularly through deficit spending, in order to narrow the gap and defer a depression. The gigantic military establishment required by Washington's foreign policy has long provided an ample outlet for such spending.

Deficit spending creates new purchasing power within the economy, along with an expanding pyramid of public and private debt. Such spending and growth of debt can convert potential depressions into recessions but invariably at the expense of inflation. Since the second world war, the United States has avoided a 1929-style depression in exchange for five recessions and a decline in the purchasing power of the dollar in every year but two.

The chronic depreciation of the dollar created another contradiction, according to Mandel, one that lies at the heart of the decline and downfall of the monetary system devised at Bretton Woods. This is the contradiction between the dollar as a means of international payments, which requires a dollar that is stable in value, and the dollar as a tool of state intervention in the economy, which requires a flexible dollar, above all a dollar that can continually inflate.

Back in 1962, Mandel in his two-volume *Traité d'Economie Marxiste* wrote: "The dilemma confronting the state in the period of capitalist decline is that of choosing between crisis and inflation. The former cannot be avoided without accentuating the latter. . . . Monetary stability—which by definition is limited in time—thus appears as the insurmountable barrier against which, in the long run, the moderating intervention of the state in the economic cycle is brought up short. The contradiction between the dollar as an anticyclical device in the United States and the dollar as money of account on the world market has already become insurmountable."[2]

In 1962, the potential seriousness of this problem was not widely recognized. The outward appearance of the dollar and the U. S. economy was still one of great strength. The economic dominance of the United States issuing from the second world war, though under challenge from Western Europe and Japan, was in some important respects actually expanding:

The biggest factor in the U. S.'s dollar drain in the early 1960s was the heavy outflow of capital (close to $4 billion a year) for foreign investment, over 40 percent of it to Western Europe.[3] This meant not only a current buildup of U. S.-owned productive assets abroad but interest and dividend income flowing back to the United States in the future. One industry after another in Europe fell under the domination of U. S. corporations as a result of this investment drive. The U. S. payments deficit was a sign of strength in another respect: it helped expand world monetary reserves in the form of dollars at a time when gold production was lagging behind the growth of world trade. An ample supply of international means of payment to finance trade was thereby assured.

In addition, the competitive position of U. S. industry as measured by labor costs was improving relative to virtually all its competitors. Between 1960 and 1965, though the once enormous productivity gap between the United States on the one hand and Europe and Japan on the other continued to narrow, the wage gap was narrowing even faster because of a more rapid rise in real wages in the latter countries. Manufacturers' labor costs in the United States actually *delined* 0.7 percent per year over this period, while the labor costs of its competitors *rose* at rates of 2 to 6 percent per year.[4] This helps explain why the surplus in the U. S. balance of trade (excess of exports over imports) increased from $4.8 billion in 1960 to a spectacular $6.6 billion in 1964.[5]

The flaw in the picture, which revealed the underlying weakness of the dollar and the Achilles' heel of the Bretton Woods system, was the tendency of foreign governments to cash in their accumulating dollar reserves for gold. This marked preference for gold was not the product of an irrational bias. Quite the contrary. The continued deficit in the U. S. balance of payments, mostly due to export of capital, overseas military spending, and foreign aid, meant that the gap between dollars held abroad and the U. S. gold reserves backing them was steadily widening. Also, because of inflation, the dollar's value in terms of what it could buy continued to decline. Its credibility as a store of value was being undermined. As U. S. gold holdings dropped (between 1960 and 1965, they declined by over $5 billion),[6] a bigger and bigger question mark arose over the dollar's as-good-as-gold status.

This contradictory situation of strength and weakness gave

way in the middle 1960s to a period of undisguised crisis for
the dollar and the international monetary system. The crisis
of the pound in 1964 and its devaluation in 1967 — an outcome of Britain's loss of empire, failure to keep its plants up
to date and in position to meet foreign competition, and a
certain resumption of overseas military commitments[7] — were
clear signs of this. Later came the gold crisis of March 1968,
the devaluation of the franc in the aftermath of the May-June
social upheaval in France, and the revaluation of the German
mark. The devaluation of the pound and franc were blows
to the dollar, because British and French exports to the United
States (as well as to other countries) became cheaper while
the prices of goods exported to these countries from the United
States rose.

The biggest blow to the dollar in the last half of the 1960s,
however, was the economic impact of the Vietnam war.

The unpopularity of the war and the existence of a highly
visible opposition to it meant that a great many Americans
were unwilling to make economic sacrifices for the war effort —
either in higher taxes or reduced real wages owing to inflation.
Congress, aware of this sentiment, put off for more than a
year passing the tax surcharge first requested by the Johnson
administration in January 1967, a delay that greatly magnified
the inflationary budget deficits in 1967 and 1968.

On the labor front, growing trade union militancy, translated
into hard-fought strikes, insured that wage increases for most
organized workers roughly kept pace with soaring prices. Thus,
hourly wages of manufacturing workers rose an average 6
percent a year in the 1965-70 period as compared to 3.7 percent in 1960-65.[8] Of course, the *real wages* of these workers,
measured in constant dollars, rose in the earlier period while
remaining level in 1965-70.

U. S. productivity in manufacturing grew only half as fast
in the later period as compared to 1960-65.[9] This also was
due in large part to effects of the Vietnam war: operation of
many industries at full capacity, reopening of less efficient
plants, lowered efficiency because of war-caused bottlenecks;
diversion of resources to war production that would otherwise have gone into productive investment, etc.

The more rapid rise in nominal wages and the slower growth
in productivity combined to reverse the favorable trend in U. S.
manufacturers' labor costs that had prevailed in the early
1960s. In 1965-70, these costs rose at an average rate of
3.9 percent per year, compared to the declining trend of the
earlier period. [10]

There were other factors that contributed to American industry's slipping competitiveness in this period. Among the most important: the imposition of wage controls and other austerity measures in Britain and other European countries, the devaluation of the pound and franc already mentioned, the continued consolidation of the Common Market, and a big merger movement among European and Japanese corporations enabling them to better compete with the U. S. giants.

The net result of all these developments was that whereas in the early sixties U. S. manufacturers were more than holding their own in world trade, after the major expansion of American involvement in the Vietnam war in 1965, their position began to slip badly. This qualitative change was graphically reflected in the U. S. trade balance, which went from a $4.7 billion surplus in 1965 [11] to a $2 billion *deficit* in 1971, [12] the first trade deficit for the United States in this century.

It was in this context that the Nixon administration instituted its first economic "game plan" and began its "Vietnamization" program. Vietnamization was mainly designed to neutralize the antiwar opposition in the United States and buy time for Nixon's war policies. But it also promised to reduce the financial drain of the war. Nixon's economic game plan called for inducing a recession by restricting credit, cutting government spending, and running a budget surplus. The administration's hope was that higher unemployment and an economic downturn would bring a reduction in wage gains being won by organized workers, enhance the competative strength of U. S. corporations, and restore the U. S. trade surplus.

The government's deflationary policies did bring a recession. In a matter of months, more than two million people were thrown out of work. Welfare rolls skyrocketed. Tight money caused housing construction to decline. Reduced tax revenues and high interest rates forced state and local governments to slash their budgets. But the recession's impact on inflation was neglible. And the continued inflation helps to explain why the rising unemployment failed to dampen labor militancy. Wage gains of organized workers continued to be substantial, though still barely keeping abreast of living costs.

In a talk on the world economic situation given in December 1969 and included in this collection, Ernest Mandel predicted that because of fears of the radicalizing effect that high unemployment would have on the working class, "as soon as the recession [in the U. S.] has reached a certain point, [the government] will revert to anti-recession measures in or-

der to limit unemployment. . . . Such a turn will intensify the
contradictions of the world capitalist system. It will deepen
the crisis of the world monetary system. It will provoke sharp
reactions among the European capitalists."

This forecast turned out to be accurate. In late 1970, the
recession and its accompanying unemployment reached the
point at which the Nixon administration decided it would be
prudent to "revert to anti-recession measures." Over the next
several months, the government acted to expand credit, lower
interest rates, provide additional tax incentives to businesses,
step up government spending, including arms spending, and
bring about a budget deficit. These measures spelled intensified inflation, an increased dollar drain, and a waning confidence in the ability of the Nixon administration to avoid
devaluing the dollar.

It wasn't long before the next part of Mandel's forecast—
a deepening crisis of the world monetary system—was realized.
The crisis was touched off May 3 and 4, 1971, by large-scale
dumping of dollars in exchange for stronger European currencies. The rush to buy marks, Swiss francs, etc. was so
massive ($1 billion in those two days in West Germany alone)
that the central banks of Germany, Belgium, Switzerland, Aus-
tria, and the Netherlands were forced to institute drastic measures, including revaluations, floating exchange rates, and
controls on capital flows, to discourage the influx of unwanted,
overvalued dollars.

These moves calmed the gathering monetary storm, but only
temporarily. Soon there was a renewed flight from the dollar
into other currencies as fears grew that a devaluation was
imminent. In late July and early August, the rush by multinational corporations, speculators, and other holders of dollars to unload turned into a stampede, and the Nixon administration was forced to act. Continued inflation of the dollar
was no longer possible within the framework of the old monetary system. Something had to be devised to take its place.

Nixon's response was his decision, announced on television
August 15, 1971, to institute wage controls; to impose a tax
surcharge on imports; to end the dollar's convertibility into
gold, allowing its exchange rate to "float," effectively devaluing
it; and to recommend further measures to prod the economy
out of recession. Most of these steps were taken under author-
ity of the Economic Stabilization Act, passed by Congress in
1970.

Nixon's sharp policy reversal underscored the gravity of
the situation. The new wage controls, whose purpose was to
sharply reduce pay increases—a goal the recession had failed

to realize, was a very risky step in that it threatened to provoke a major political confrontation between labor and the government. The breakdown of the international monetary system threatened a severe disruption of world trade and the possibility of an open trade war. As an editorial in the September 25, 1971, *Business Week* explained, "In such a trade war, major industries would be wrecked, billions of dollars worth of investments destroyed, and the whole fabric of peaceful, profitable commercial relations built up in the past 25 years torn to shreds. . . ."

After more than three months of confusion and uncertainty in international commerce and after hard bargaining between representatives of the "Group of Ten" (the ten most powerful capitalist nations), a compromise agreement on a realignment of currencies was negotiated December 18, 1971, at the Smithsonian Institution in Washington, D. C. The agreement reflected the new relationship of forces that had developed among these powers, in which the U. S. — though still the most powerful — had suffered a relative decline. The currency realignment involved an effective devaluation of the dollar against all the leading currencies of 12 percent, including an 8.6 percent formal devaluation of the dollar (through an increase in the official price of gold) and a revaluation of the mark and the yen.

The dollar devaluation cheapened U. S. exports while making foreign goods more expensive on the U. S. market, thereby offsetting to some extent U. S. industry's declining competitiveness. On the other hand, the devaluation could be expected to discourage U. S. capital exports, since the cost in dollars of setting up or expanding factories, banking facilities, and retail outlets abroad increased as a result.

A very serious effect of the devaluation was the heavy loss it caused every country that held large quantities of dollars in its reserves. This was a blow to the dollar's role as a reserve currency: in the future, central banks would be less willing to hold dollars. This role was further weakened by the fact that the new agreement did not restore the convertibility of the dollar into gold.

Although President Nixon hailed the new accord as "the most significant monetary agreement in the history of the world," an editorial in the December 20, 1971, *New York Times* took a somewhat more sober view: "All the basic issues involved in rebuilding the international monetary system . . . remain to be solved. Meanwhile, the world is on what might be called an inconvertible dollar standard — and it remains to be seen how stable that system will be."

A number of monetary experts have argued that the international monetary system could be put on a sound footing if the dollar was replaced by a newly created international reserve currency that would have no circulation in any national economy but would be used only by central banks. They argue that such a currency, if correctly administered by some sort of world council of finance ministers, would avoid the fatal flaw of the dollar or any other national currency: chronic inflation.

Mandel's answer is that this solution "would be a complete utopia. The realization of such a program presupposes the existence of a world capitalist government independent of the great imperialist powers; that is, the disappearance of inter-imperialist competition. But it is precisely the exacerbation of that competition that has been manifested since the opening of the monetary crisis." 13

Other reforms have been proposed by monetary experts in recent years. These include a return to the gold standard (advocated by Jacques Rueff, former adviser to de Gaulle), a large increase in the price of gold, and a unification of the Common Market currencies and their use as reserve money. In the last article of this collection, Mandel takes up all these reforms and explains why in his opinion none of them can resolve the monetary crisis.

Mandel, in fact, sees no solution to the monetary crisis within the framework of capitalism. He thinks the decline of the dollar is far from over: "The Bretton Woods system lasted twenty-five years, the last five years in death agony. The system born in Washington will not survive a decade. The next recession or the next social explosion in an important imperialist country threatens to precipitate its decomposition." 14

Periodic recessions are inevitable, as the experience of the last twenty-five years demonstrates. Among the factors Mandel sees creating the basis for social explosions are the intensifying efforts of the major capitalist powers to expand their shares of the world market and increase corporate profits through speedup schemes, government-sponsored attacks on wages, and growing restrictions on workers' right to strike.

The present monetary system may not by the only casualty of future social explosions. If an adequate revolutionary leadership is created, says Mandel, such explosions can lead to capitalism itself being abolished and to the victory of socialism on a world scale.

JON BRITTON

June 1972

Chronology

1944

July — The World Monetary Conference meets in Bretton Woods, New Hampshire, with forty-four governments participating.

1960

October — Washington announces that potential claims on United States gold by holders of dollars abroad now exceeds the U. S. supply. The report sparks speculative buying on the London gold market.

November 16 — President Eisenhower orders the Defense Department to reduce the number of dependents of military personnel living in other countries from 484,000 to 200,000.

November 19 — Treasury Secretary Robert Anderson and Undersecretary Douglas Dillon fly to Europe to discuss the balance of payments problem. They ask the West German government for $600 million to help meet the costs of stationing U. S. troops in Germany but are turned down.

1961

February 6 — President Kennedy tells Congress that strengthening the economy and expanding exports is the best solution to the balance of payments problem. He also recommends that the value of goods American tourists are allowed to bring back from abroad duty-free be slashed from $500 to $100.

August 10 — Britain applies for membership in the Common Market.

1962

January 25 — President Kennedy submits the Trade Expansion Act of 1962 to Congress. Its subsequent passage opens the way for the "Kennedy Round" of talks aimed at worldwide tariff reductions.

December 21 — President Kennedy and British Prime Minister Harold Macmillan, meeting in Nassau, announce that they have agreed on "the development of a multilateral NATO nuclear force in the closest consultation with other NATO allies."

1963

January — The French government vetoes British entry into the Common Market. Afterwards, the British pound comes under speculative attack. The pound is successfully defended by the Bank of England thanks to a $250 million loan from U. S. and other central banks.

July 18 — President Kennedy in a special message to Congress asks for an "interest equalization tax" designed to curb the outflow of capital, reduce the balance of payments deficit, and slow the loss of U. S. gold.

1964

October-November — Faced by a worsening trade and payments deficit, the new British Labour government announces a 15 percent surcharge on imports of manufactured goods and measures to "modernize" and improve the competitiveness of British industry. Rather than firming up the pound in money markets, however, the announcement triggers large-scale conversion of pounds into other, stronger currencies.

November 25 — Britain obtains a $3 billion loan from U. S. and European central banks for use in supporting the pound.

1965

February 10 — In a special message to Congress, President Johnson asks for voluntary cooperation by American business and banking to reduce their lending and investing abroad as a means of reducing the U. S. balance of payments deficit. He also asks Congress to reduce from $100 to $50 the duty-free exemption on purchases abroad by American tourists.

1966

November 29 — President Johnson announces a $5.6 billion cut in federal programs delayed or cancelled because of the skyrocketing costs of the Vietnam war.

1967

January 10 — President Johnson asks for a 6 percent tax surcharge to help meet rising Vietnam war costs.

May 2 — It is announced that the United States and Great Britain will trim NATO forces by 41,500 troops in 1968. The U. S. troop reduction of 30,000 will, it is anticipated, reduce the U. S. balance of payments deficit by $100 million a year.

August 3 — President Johnson asks for a 10 percent surcharge on income taxes to fund the Vietnam war, his request for a tax increase in January having been bottled up in Congress.

November 2 — Calling it "the end of the imperial era," Britain's Foreign Secretary George Brown announces that Britain will withdraw its armed forces from certain areas in the Mideast.

November 18 — The Labour government devalues the British pound, lowering its parity from $2.80 to $2.40.

1968

January 1 — President Johnson places restrictions on American investment abroad and introduces a program to curb American travel to Europe, cut down on government spending abroad, and stimulate U. S. exports.

January 16 — British Prime Minister Harold Wilson announces the complete withdrawal of British troops from the Far East and Persian Gulf by 1971 and a new austerity program, all designed to "make devaluation work."

March — An International gold buying fever hits the markets of the world March 1, fed by the fear and belief that the U. S. will be unable to maintain the $35-an-ounce price of gold. By March 15 massive buying pushes the price of gold in the Paris market to an all-time high of $44.36 an ounce. The London Gold Pool members meet in Washington March 17 to face the crisis of their rapidly dwindling gold reserves and agree that all gold transactions between governments will continue at $35 an ounce, but that they will no longer sell gold on the private market. Thus, a "two-tier" price system for gold is established: fluctuating prices in the private markets, and the fixed $35 per ounce price for official monetary transactions.

May 1 — The "Kennedy Round" tariff reductions are rescheduled to aid the U. S. balance of payments.

May-June — Massive protests by French students combine with the rising discontent of French workers and farmers to produce the biggest general strike ever.

November — Another gold crisis breaks out, triggered by large-scale speculation on an anticipated revaluation of the German mark and a devaluation of the French franc.

1969

January — The U. S. Department of Labor reports that the inflation rate is the worst since 1951. The Commerce Department says that the U. S. trade surplus the previous year was the lowest since the Great Depression. The Treasury Department announces that it will have to pay the highest interest rate since the Civil War.

March 7 — The price of gold climbs to record levels, pushed by speculation that the French franc is about to topple and fears of renewed labor struggles in France.

May 5 — Britain announces its intention to renew its drive for full membership in the European Common Market now that de Gaulle, the chief foe of British entry, has retired.

June 9 — Interest rates rise to new highs in an atmosphere of mounting crisis in the U. S. financial markets.

July 24 — After five years of negotiations, agreement is reached on creating Special Drawing Rights (SDRs), the first internationally managed reserve asset.

August 8 — The French franc is devalued 12.5 percent in relation to the dollar. The devaluation was triggered by massive losses of French gold and dollar reserves.

September 2 — President Nixon, to slow the economy, orders a 75 percent reduction in new contracts for federal government construction and urges local and state governments to cut back on construction projects funded jointly with federal funds.

October 6 — It is announced that the U. S. unemployment rate rose steeply to 4 percent in September, indicating that President Nixon's recession-inducing policies are beginning to take effect.

October 24 — Chancellor Willy Brandt's Social Democratic-led government, in its first major act, revalues the German mark upward 9.3 percent.

1970

June 21 — Tight money, mismanagement, a huge debt, and

the diversion of capital into various speculative schemes combine to force the Penn Central Railroad into bankruptcy.

December 1 — The ten European members of NATO agree on a $1 billion "defense improvement program" to ease the financial strain of NATO on the United States.

December 4 — The U. S. Labor Department announces that the November unemployment rate was 5.8 percent, the highest level in seven and one-half years.

1971

January 7 — In one of the first moves aimed at pulling the U. S. economy out of its fifth post-World War II recession, the Federal Reserve lowers the rate at which it lends money to member banks, bringing that rate to its lowest level in nine years.

January 8 — The U. S. Labor Department announces that the unemployment rate reached 6 percent in December, the highest level in nine years.

March 11 — President Nixon urges legislation limiting textile imports.

May 9 — In an effort to get rid of unwanted dollars, four European countries led by West Germany revalue their currencies. The West German mark is allowed to float within undisclosed limits.

July 27 — U. S. monetary reserves declined by $307 million in June to $13.5 billion, the lowest level since 1938, it is announced. Secretary of Commerce Maurice Stans warns Congress that the U. S. might have a trade deficit in 1971 for the first time in this century.

August 4 — The French central bank announces measures designed to stem a speculative flow of dollars into France. This sets off panic selling of dollars in Zurich, Frankfurt, and London.

August 7 — A congressional subcommittee headed by Wisconsin Democrat Henry S. Reuss states that the dollar is "overvalued" in relation to other currencies and should be devalued one way or another. The announcement is followed by a renewed speculative flow of funds out of the dollar and into various European currencies.

August 13 — The dollar weakens further in chaotic trading on world currency exchanges as bankers in New York say privately that a breakdown of the system of fixed exchange rates negotiated at Bretton Woods in 1944 appears to be imminent.

August 15 — President Nixon announces his "New Economic Policy," including an end to the dollar's convertibility into gold effectively devaluing it, a wage freeze, a tax surcharge

on imports, and further measures to prod the economy out
of recession.

August 23 — For the first time since Nixon's August 15 speech,
European money markets reopen, with a hodgepodge of
fixed and floating exchange rates.

December 18 — After months of great uncertainty in international commerce and finance, the ten most powerful capitalist powers reach an agreement on a general realignment
of currencies, including a devaluation of the dollar, at the
Smithsonian Institution in Washington, D. C. The agreement
does not restore the convertibility of the dollar into gold.

1972

January 13 — The dollar falls to a record low against the
West German mark and weakens against other major currencies as Europe's money centers are swept by anxieties
over the durability of the previous month's currency realignment.

March 9 — The dollar is hit by fresh rounds of selling in international money markets as the Dutch national bank announces a tightening of foreign exchange controls to restrain
the influx of unwanted dollars and as rumors of impending
moves of a similar kind by other countries circulate. Treasury
Secretary John Connally states that the United States will
not even discuss the restoration of convertibility of the dollar.

Part 1

Wilson's Quid Pro Quo
With World Imperialism

From the December 5, 1964, issue of World Outlook, *predecessor of* Intercontinental Press. *This weekly newsmagazine describes itself as specializing "in political analysis and interpretation of events of particular interest to the labor, socialist, colonial independence, Black, and women's liberation movements."*

For the past half century, it has been a general rule that social democratic governments, or those led by social democrats, in the major countries of Western Europe are brought down sooner or later by national and international finance capital after they have completed the function they were designed for in the eyes of the bourgeoisie. This happened to the Herman Mueller government in Germany in 1930 and to Ramsay MacDonald's Labour government in 1931. The downfall of the first Leon Blum ("popular front") government in 1937 was a classical example.

During mid-November, the pattern seemed to be repeating itself in Great Britain. The Labour cabinet of Harold Wilson appeared to be the target of a vast conspiracy mounted by the "faceless bankers of Zurich." In other words, it looked like international finance capital had decided to force down the pound. For a few hours it almost seemed that they had won and that Wilson would have to devaluate and devaluate heavily. (Optimists among the capitalists even added that he would have to form a coalition with the Liberal Party.)

Then a strange thing happened. Whereas *private* international finance capital had been gnawing away at the pound and the Wilson cabinet, *"public"* international finance capital rushed to the aid of the beleaguered Wilson and the British pound. Within a few hours, the governors and boards of directors of the U. S. Federal Reserve System, the German Bundesbank, the Banque de France, the Italian, Swiss, Dutch, Belgian, and Swedish national banks, poured hundreds of millions of dollars into the British treasury. All told, Wilson was handed a purse of $3 billion — and the pound was saved.

Why this strange behavior, which doesn't seem to correspond at all to the rules of international capital? Have the international bankers suddenly become reconciled with socialism, if it is "introduced at a snail's pace" in accordance with the credo of the British Labour Party bureaucrats? Or does the dramatic operation prove that in the eyes of the international bourgeoisie Wilson is really "a better servant of capitalism than the Tories," as a few fossilized ultralefts in Britain maintain, and therefore worthy of a really big gold medal?

Despite the attractive simplicity, neither line of reasoning is satisfactory. The international central banks are neither going socialist nor rewarding Wilson for being more capitalist than the Tories. In the first place, the international monetary system governing the capitalist world economy today is a very delicate and vulnerable structure. Under the gold exchange standard, the currencies of all capitalist countries (except the United States) are covered by gold and U. S. dollars. Through this system, the "creeping inflation" characteristic of contemporary capitalism in countries like the U. S. and Britain is spread over the whole world system. This is the price capitalism had to pay for the possibility of slowing down the rate of crises due to overproduction and transforming big crises into "smaller" recessions. As a result of this permanent inflationary trend, all currencies today are both highly vulnerable and tightly interlinked.

The New York, Frankfort, and Paris central bankers feared — and rightly so — that devaluation of the pound would be rapidly followed by a general breakdown of the present exchange rates of all currencies and by contraction of international trade which, under the present conditions of slowdown of economic expansion in Western Europe (with a recession in Italy and near stagnation in France), could precipitate a full-scale economic crisis. In rushing to the defense of the pound, they didn't act out of love for Harold Wilson. They had their own interests in mind.

Secondly, the Wilson Labour government has hardly fulfilled the task which capitalism has designated for it, a task inherent in the Labour program of accepting the capitalist state as the limiting frame for projected reforms. The job laid out for the Labour government is to get the British working class to accept what the Tories have notoriously been unable to impose: namely, wage restraints. To topple Wilson through a conspiracy of finance capital *before* the unions have been inveigled into accepting a restrictive "incomes policy" would most certainly provoke sharp radicalization of the British Labour movement. Wall Street, Frankfurt, and Paris are not that stupid. They try to estimate the relationship of class forces in Britain in a realistic way.

Thirdly — and this should be noted most carefully — the $3 billion windfall for Wilson was not one-sided. It was a quid pro quo. In return for a strengthened financial hand, Wilson betrayed some of his most emphatic promises in the field of foreign policy. In the *very same week* in which the world's central banks came to his rescue with a big purse, Wilson made three momentous decisions in complete contradiction to the avowed foreign policy of the Labour party.

1) He decided, after all, to carry out the Tory agreement to sell Buccaneer planes to South Africa's fascist-like Prime Minister Verwoerd, thereby strengthening the apartheid regime. How scandalous this decision was can be judged from the fact that the conservative-liberal weekly *The Economist* favored canceling the contract for moral reasons!

2) He extended the facilities of Ascension Island to the U. S. and Belgian governments for their counterrevolutionary paratrooper operation against the Stanleyville government, thereby becoming an accomplice in the imperialist aggression against the Congolese revolution. He even went so far as to publicly approve this infamous move.

3) He suddenly reversed his stand on MLF (NATO's multilateral nuclear force) and the Nassau agreement, agreeing to continue construction of three submarines to be armed with Polaris missiles equipped with nuclear warheads, agreeing to consider setting up a special NATO fleet equipped with nuclear weapons (to which his government would eventually add the three submarines under construction on condition that veto rights are maintained on use of the nuclear weapons), and agreeing even to integrate the West German Bundeswehr, with its Nazi-trained and Nazi-inspired high command, in the proposed NATO nuclear force!

The proposals in which Wilson has now acquiesced constitute direct military threats against the Soviet Union and the East European workers' states.

The three betrayals are sizable. They provide help for the international bourgeoisie in some very difficult situations. They cast additional revealing light on the alacrity with which $3 billion was rounded up for the Bank of England.

Revolutionary Marxists in Britain and elsewhere are duty bound to denounce and oppose these betrayals. But in doing so they should not descend to mere name calling or make the gross error of considering a Labour government and a Tory government as equivalents. Lenin long ago pointed out in his treatise on the infantile disorder of ultraleftism that the overwhelming majority of the British working class consider the Labour party to be *their* party and a Labour government to be *their* government, as is indeed the case since the Labour movement is based on the trade unions. This reality cannot be disregarded by any British Marxist seeking to win mass influence. The penalty for brushing it aside is political isolation.

Wilson's course must be carefully analyzed into its components so that his actual betrayals stand out clearly. In the current instance, Wilson's betrayals involve the foreign policy which the British workers were led to believe would be followed if Labour were elected. His departures from this policy must be denounced.

What the Labour government requires, if it is to win re-election by a thumping majority, is a foreign policy that will arouse enthusiasm and hope among the workers and their allies not only in Britain but throughout the world. It must be demanded that the Labour government initiate a genuine socialist policy. In the instances before us, this would include an effective boycott of Verwoerd's apartheid regime, sincere moves toward an alliance with the African revolution, and energetic moves towards unilateral nuclear disarmament.

If these demands are put in a reasoned way, with careful emphasis on the basic difference between a Labour government and a Tory government, the vanguard of the British workers will understand and begin the process of mobilizing appropriate action to rectify matters.

November 30, 1964

De Gaulle Doesn't Know It
But the Golden Days of Capitalism Are Over

From the February 19, 1965, issue of World Outlook.

On Thursday, February 4, 1965, General de Gaulle made a proposal that created a minor sensation in the stock exchanges and editorial staffs of the big daily papers throughout the world. He suggested that the United States, Great Britain, Canada, Australia, West Germany, Japan, Italy, Belgium, Holland, Switzerland, Sweden—that is, the main imperialist centers—should go back to the gold standard. And a few days later, on Saturday, February 13, he topped this proposal by a unilateral decision to put France back on the gold standard; i.e., to make up its deficit in the balance of payments with all capitalist countries in gold and only gold.

Most bourgeois economists and the main central banks of the capitalist world didn't take de Gaulle's proposal very seriously. In fact, only *Pravda* declared with a straight face that it sounded "reasonable."

Under the gold standard, any debt which one country finds itself owing another as a result of current exchanges (in goods, tourist trade, capital imports and exports, etc.) must be paid in gold. Any deficit in the current balance of payments leads, therefore, to an outflow of gold. But the same system also means that currency must be exchangeable in gold. An outflow of gold therefore automatically involves a reduction in the existing volume of money inside the country. Bourgeois economists and capitalist governments have known since 1929—they learned it the hard way!—that to reduce the volume of money circulation means reducing the volume of aggregate demand for goods and services in a country; i.e., reducing the volume of employment, income, and production—that is, precipitating a depression.

To demand going back to the gold standard means in fact to demand going back to the laissez-faire economy of liberal capitalism in which market forces adjust supply and demand *in the long run* through the mechanism of prices, in which the inflow and outflow of gold distributes gold reserves among

25

the different countries *in the long run* more or less in proportion to their productive capacity or wealth. These "adjustments" are brought about automatically. This is what admirers of the gold standard like Jacques Rueff, de Gaulle's adviser in monetary matters, consider to be so excellent.

However, the adjustments are not brought about in a "gradual," harmonious way, but through sharp breaks and discontinuities in the system. Before demand "readjusts" to a new level of supply, the phenomenon called "overproduction" appears. And before the outflow of gold "readjusts" the balance of payments, the phenomenon known as "deflation" occurs. Both have the unfortunate tendency of creating more and more unemployment, sharper and sharper cuts in production, and greater and greater social crises in a world where capitalism has ceased to expand as a global system, where it finds itself instead in continual struggle with revolutions, workers' states, and masses of people who openly challenge the merits of the system and who want to replace it with a system in which conscious planning takes the place of the "blind man's cane" of the market forces.

Because of this, there is not the slightest chance that de Gaulle's proposal will be taken up. It would be suicide for capitalism to return to a rigid system of money and credit controlled automatically by the supply of gold. Such a system could lead only to a major depression.

Those who advocate returning to the gold standard score a good point when they argue that the present monetary system leads to increasing inflation. This is completely correct. But increasing inflation is the only means by which a capitalist economy can convert grave depressions into "minor" recessions. What capitalist government in the United States, for instance, would risk having fifteen or twenty million unemployed for the sake of "fighting inflation" or "going back to the gold standard"?

There are many supplementary reasons showing how irrational it would be to return to the classic gold standard in the present world situation. The two main gold-producing countries are South Africa and the Soviet Union. To return to the gold standard would mean opening the most delicately complex and explosive segment of the present world capitalist economy — the international monetary system — to the manipulations of Hendryk Verwoerd and Brezhnev-Kosygin, none of whom are exactly respected figures in banking circles. Consequently, de Gaulle's proposal strikes the average bourgeois economist or capitalist politician as nothing but a joke of the sick variety.

For many years the annual increase in gold production has lagged behind the increase in the volume of world trade and world production of manufactured goods. Even a sharp increase in the price of gold, say doubling or tripling it, would not fundamentally change that situation, although it would represent a handsome gift of many billions of dollars to the Soviet Union which could then double or triple purchases in the capitalist countries on the basis of current gold production. A permanent crisis of international liquidity would ensue, bringing great unhappiness throughout the capitalist world — with the exception of the hoarders of gold. Indeed Rueff's (and de Gaulle's) wisdom in this field comes closer to the prejudices of the classical French peasant (who finds it a comfort to sleep on a mattress in which a few pieces of gold are hidden) than to the views of academic economists, let alone Marxist economic science (notwithstanding *Pravda's* approving comments).

But if de Gaulle's proposal has no chance whatsoever of being accepted, it has nonetheless caused great uneasiness and worry among central banks, especially in New York and London. And if it hasn't brought about much of a rise in the price of South African gold mine stocks and bonds, it has certainly increased the general's nuisance value in the eyes of the rather nervous and harassed Johnson administration.

For it is a fact that the present monetary system of the capitalist world — the so-called "gold exchange standard" — is at present experiencing a severe crisis. Under this system, a central bank can cover its currency in either of two ways: in gold or in certain "privileged" currencies like dollars and pounds. This means that when the USA owes money to another country (shows a deficit in its balance of payments with that country), it need not make up the balance in gold; it can pay in dollars. But this also means that the dollars accumulating in central (and private) banks everywhere in the world "because they are as good as gold," must be exchangeable for gold at any time at the American central bank, the Federal Reserve System.

The "gold exchange standard" could function perfectly well as long as all capitalist coutries outside the USA were dollar hungry due to the shortage of goods and capital in the postwar period which only the USA could supply, and as long as these countries had adverse balances of payment with the USA. But these "golden days" of the dollar empire, following the "golden days" of unmanipulated currencies governed solely by market forces are gone forever. They came to an end in the middle fifties when the great boom in Western Europe and

Japan started, when these areas began to build up large dollar balances, and when the USA found itself running into a continual deficit in its balance of payments, thereby opening up the flow of gold from Fort Knox in their direction.

The deficit in the American balance of payments is a complex phenomenon. At one and the same time it expresses both the *increasing strength* of the competitors of the U. S. and the still *great superiority* of the U. S. over these competitors. For the final cause of this deficit in the balance of payments is the increasing *export of U. S. capital* to other countries where the rate of profit is higher than in the U. S. due to the fact that the organic composition of capital remains lower (i.e., automation is less advanced) and the rate of exploitation of labor higher (i.e., wages are lower).

The export of American capital to the Common Market countries constituted America's "secret weapon," with which Wall Street neutralized the advantages the European capitalists sought to gain for themselves by building up this preference zone for their goods. As a matter of fact, what de Gaulle is really aiming at is to stop this continual flow of American capital into Europe which has now reached the point where key plants in most European countries have already been taken over by American monopolies. (On the European continent, every significant capitalist company in the vital computer-production sector is controlled by U. S. interests.)

Because of the export of U. S. capital and the constant outflow of gold from the USA, the balance between the remaining stock of gold at Fort Knox and the current deficits favoring other countries has become quite delicate. In fact, total U. S. obligations to private and public institutions in other countries are higher today than the total gold stock in the U. S. This means that if all foreign central and private banks were at one and the same time to demand payment, and payment in gold only, not dollars, the U. S. would lose all its gold and the dollar would collapse.

Of course, this will not happen. Most of the central banks involved must defend currencies bound as tightly to the dollar and its fate as their capitalism is to U. S. capitalism and its prosperity. But it would be sufficient for *some* creditors to demand payment in gold instead of dollars to have a quite undue influence on the present very unstable balance on which the dollar sits. And since de Gaulle's France holds precisely this position of a minor creditor, it is able to that degree to make a nuisance of itself, blackmailing Washington into paying ransom in fields as distant as the Multilateral Force, nuclear secrets and the setting up of a "NATO directorate."

The dollar is vulnerable not only because of the current deficit in the U. S. balance of payments. In fact, under the "gold exchange standard," this deficit is merely a way of spreading credit inflation from the U. S. to other capitalist countries, thereby "exporting" American "prosperity," including its shaky foundation of increasing indebtedness.

The dollar is also vulnerable because of the constant erosion of its purchasing power in the U. S. itself. Inflation in the U. S. is not "imported" through the gold exchange standard; it is rooted in the huge volume of public debt and unproductive expenses (twenty-five years of uninterrupted "boom" based on military expenditures!) as well as in a staggering amount of private indebtedness. To destroy these roots would mean destroying the very factor which up to now has prevented a new depression of the 1929 type.

Thus President Johnson recently solemnly pledged that if the threat of a new recession appears in 1965, he will immediately make new tax cuts; i.e., increase government "deficit financing" and "deficit spending" (fancy names for inflation).

To impose the gold standard would have the effect of suppressing the deficit in the balance of payments and rooting up domestic inflation. But the price would be the utter ruination of American and world capitalism today. That's why the world capitalist structure can't afford to return to a "stable" currency and the "golden" days of its youth. Those days are gone forever.

The Pound Sterling Bows Out
as the Queen of Moneys

From the December 8, 1967, issue of World Outlook. *Written in response to the November 18, 1967, devaluation of the British pound.*

Several historic tendencies met at the crossroads in the devaluation of the pound sterling. The most important, without doubt, were the decline of British imperialism on the one hand and the growing social crisis in Great Britain on the other. The British Labour Party chiefs, good doctors at the bedside of capitalism, tried for a long time to bolster the patient by means of stimulants. But in face of the gravity of the relapse, they could not avoid the surgery which many experts had desired for quite some time.

For a century, from the battle of Waterloo until the shots fired at Sarajevo, the pound sterling was the queen of the world. Not that all the gold flowed toward the City, London's financial district, often there was more in Paris and sometimes even in Petrograd.

What gave the pound sterling its power was the superiority of British industry, the rise in productivity which it enjoyed in relation to that of other countries, the low prices which enabled it to penetrate all customs barriers, the abundance of capital which flowed toward all continents.

This abundance was such that the returns on capital invested abroad, for more than a half century, from 1885 to 1939, outweighed the capital exported annually.

The British bourgeoisie constructed the Empire to assure the security of their investments. They planted naval and military bases throughout the world to defend this empire and — prudent stockholders — spent for this only a fraction of the income returned by the capital invested abroad. Another function of the Empire was to extort from the colonized peoples — above all those of India and Egypt — payment for a good part of the costs of maintaining the British army, fleet, and administration.

Two victorious wars and a wave of colonial revolution completely undermined the solidity of the edifice. A good part of the investments abroad had to be liquidated to finance the war effort. The political independence granted most of the former colonized countries meant that while the British investments were still safe, these countries hardly contributed any longer to financing the Establishment of her Gracious Majesty. The revenue brought in by these investments is still considerable, but their proportion in relation to the national income has been greatly reduced. They no longer suffice to absorb the traditional deficit of Britain's trade balance; above all they are insufficient to finance the military effort which this weakened imperialist structure continues to require in all quarters of the globe.

The worst is that Great Britain long ago lost its monopoly in the world market on high productivity. Taking into account only the capitalist countries, the United States, Western Germany, and Japan stand above England's technical level and sell industrial products at a lower price. In this is to be found the definitive cause of the continual deficit in the trade balance, the fundamental reason why the pound sterling no longer serves as an international means of payment.

For two decades, the Labour and Conservative governments succeeding each other in office have sought to hide this fundamental truth. In line with this, they have imposed many useless sacrifices on the British people. The day of reckoning finally came. The pound sterling is dead as the queen of moneys. The sterling zone is dying. The pound is becoming one money among others, standing somewhere between the deutsche mark and the Italian lira. Thus the economic and financial reality, like a faithful seismograph, registered this major political overturn — the irreparable decline of British imperialism.

Not since the general strike of 1926 has the British working class been beaten in a direct struggle — something unique in all of Europe. It suffered, it is true, the upset of MacDonald's split in 1931. [1] But its Labour Party came out of this holding the bulk of its forces, accentuating its socialist doctrine, remaining more than ever the symbol and rallying point of the world of labor as opposed to the world of capital.

This undefeated working class assembled the majority of the nation in 1945 in hope of constructing a socialist society along the peaceful road. If ever this hope could seem realistic anywhere, it was certainly at that moment and in this country.

It is not easy to see what social force could have stood in the way of the Labour Party forces at that time when they sought to definitively break with the capitalist regime.

The leadership didn't want socialism. Of course, they passed the most progressive social legislation, they nationalized some uneconomic branches of industry, but they left the monopoly of the manufacturing industries in the hands of the private capitalists and left it up to them to introduce the most modern technology in current production.

The results were not long in becoming manifest. The British economy showed a rate of growth below that of its main competitors. To seek to adjust high social expenses with an economy based on private profit—this has long been impossible under capitalism. Thus first came the austerity which led to the discontent of a part of the middle classes and the white-collar workers, permitting the Conservatives to return to power. Then came fifteen years of Tory power during which the old industrial position was progressively wasted away in luxury expenditures and the growing flight of capital. Competitive capacities deteriorated more and more, not because wages were too high but because productive investments were insufficient.

To step these up, it was necessary—as this course logically implied—to stimulate and subsidize profits; and in order to accomplish this, to reduce social costs and real wages. If the Tories had tried this, there would have been a general strike. Thus the job was left to Harold Wilson, greeted by the British capitalist press as the champion of "modernization" of the country from the time of his election.

Wilson loyally applied the program of capitalist health improvements. He reinstated austerity, levied new taxes on consumers' goods, froze wages, threatened organizers of strikes with criminal prosecution. Undoubtedly he scored the success of a surprise attack. For a year the British workers remained stupefied at the spectacle of "their" representatives, whom they had lifted into office at the cost of such efforts and sacrifices, unmasking themselves as worse enemies than the representatives of the bosses had ever dared show themselves in forty years.

But after this year of paralysis, came a second year of anger. One after the other, the big unions, the labor army by entire detachments, revolted against Harold Wilson. The Transport Workers were the first to take the road of revolt; Wilson was beaten at the last Trades Union Congress. A shameful bit of skullduggery still saved him at the Labour Congress at Scarborough—he promised the miners to suspend closing down the pits for the time being, without adding that this promise implied the perspective of an accelerated shutdown in the spring. The Miners Union thus voted for him at Scarborough; but when they discovered how they had been cheated (Lord Robens, the head of the nationalized coal mines, charged the government with seeking to reduce employment in the mines from 380,000 persons to 65,000 within a time limit of a few years), they turned violently against the cabinet. Then the Amalgamated Engineering Union elected a militant of the left, a former Communist, Hugh Scanlon, to replace an extreme right-wing bureaucrat as main leader of the organization. Next came some very spirited and militant strikes in the ports of London and Liverpool.

Already cut off from the majority of the trade union movement, Wilson had to undergo a furious assault from almost the whole party when his chancellor of the exchequer, James Callaghan, publicly supported a declaration made by the governor of the Bank of England, Sir Leslie O'Brien, according to which a permanent pool of unemployed is indispensable if Britain is to overcome inflation. This signified abandoning the principle of full employment, which has dominated the reformist ideology since the crisis of 1929. This was the drop that made the cup flow over. Wilson was threatened with a revolt by his whole party. This is what led him to devaluate.

The truth was that the economic policy of the Labour cabinet was caught in a dilemma: it sought at any price to wipe out the deficit in the balance of payments; and it sought at the same time to step up the economy. The struggle against the deficit in foreign payments implied deflation; deflation implied mounting unemployment (at present it is without doubt around 800,000). But to seek at one and the same time to carry out deflation and to step up production is an impossible combination. By devaluing, that is, by cutting export prices 17 percent, Wilson can hope to stimulate production and discourage imports; i.e., reestablish equilibrium in the balance of payments without choking off industrial expansion. The immediate effect will be to cut down unemployment and weaken the pressure on the cabinet from the trade unions.

But the respite will not last long inasmuch as Great Britain imports a large part of its food and raw materials. Devaluation stimulates not only exports (and thus production); it also provokes a rise in import prices, hence a rise in the cost of living. The specialists estimate this at 4 percent; no doubt their figure is too low. Wilson will seek to block the demands for an increase in wages. Cousins[2] and Scanlon, under the pressure of their rank and file, have already warned him that he should be under no illusions about this.

If the government seeks to impose a new wage freeze, the battle it evaded in the field of unemployment will have to be conducted in the field of incomes. If it concedes in this, inflation will become all the worse.

As always, the devaluation will thus provide only a brief respite, after which all the unresolved problems will reappear, sharper than ever.

In the international domain, the capitalist countries were happy over Wilson's "moderation"; if he had devalued 30 percent, it would have rudely shaken their markets. In exchange for this "moderation," they granted him a bit of charity in the form of a loan. The editorial writer of *The Economist* summed up perfectly the relations between the British bourgeoisie and their foreign partners in the title: "Beggars or Choosers." Are we beggars, or people who still have a choice? The weekend of November 18 provided an answer to the question.

Aside from the British colonies and semicolonies, the only countries that immediately devaluated their own currencies following the devaluation of the pound sterling were those, such as Spain and Israel, that have an analogous domestic problem of simultaneous inflation and stagnation. The operation on their part had a political rather than monetary motive.

In Brussels there was exultation: Great Britain's path toward the Common Market was singularly shortened by the elimination of two obstacles: the international role of sterling and the economic stagnation of Great Britain. It remains to be seen whether the social crisis and industrial competition will not yet arouse sentiments of a different kind among the capitalists of Western Europe.

For if in truth the other imperialist moneys are, to say the least, technically solid, the real problem does not lie there. The devaluation of the pound places a discount on British exports. If the world market is expanding, this discount brings a loss to no one. If it is stagnating, other countries are threatened with paying the bill for the temporary advantages assured to the British industrialists.

The first to become worried were the Japanese, who for the moment are experiencing the greatest expansion. In New York and Dusseldorf, the reaction is like that of the primitive rainmakers: "May a recession be staved off! May an expansion come!" The fate of the international capitalist economy will be determined in the next six months. If in Germany a recovery sets in, the threat of a general recession will be avoided. . .

this time. If the recession in Germany lasts, the effects of this recession and the British devaluation will make 1968 a somber year for the international capitalist economy. A touch of fever could lead some of the other capitalist powers to take advantage in their turn of devaluation in order to get out of a decline. The whole international monetary system threatens to be shaken.

The root of the problem is to be found here. Like the pound sterling, the dollar, keystone of the arch of the entire world monetary system, has a double function requiring two qualities that are becoming more and more contradictory. As a means of international payment, it must be as stable as possible. As a weapon of struggle against a crisis in the United States (and by way of ricochet for the international capitalist economy!) it must also be flexible, that is, as unstable as possible. Any return to the automatism of the gold standard threatens to precipitate a grave economic crisis, which the capitalist world must avoid at any cost. But any continual monetary manipulation for expansionist aims is certain to precipitate inflation and the erosion of the international monetary system. The main lesson of the devaluation of the pound is that within the framework of the capitalist regime, there is no way out of this dilemma.

The Dollar Crisis I

From the January 19, 1968, issue of World Outlook.

A country's economic strength, in the last analysis, is always a function of its productive capacity and labor productivity, that is, of its potential for producing a given quantity of products with the smallest possible expenditure of labor. In a capitalist regime, this potential can be measured by the per capita value of production and by commodity prices relative to those of other countries (that is by the competitive capacity of industry and agriculture).

From this standpoint, the United States remains by far the most powerful and prosperous capitalist country in the world. Furthermore, the gap separating the U. S. from its principal competitors and from the USSR, which had tended to shrink between 1950 and 1960, has again widened in recent years.

How can the "dollar crisis" be explained under these circumstances? What is its basis? Does it reveal a structural weakness in the American economy, or does it instead show its strength?

At first glance, the cause of the "dollar crisis" appears self-evident: it's the U. S. balance-of-payments deficit. When a country has a deficit in its balance of payments, that means that the sum of the resources which it acquires in a year's time (commodity imports; services purchased abroad; purchase of stock or other foreign paper) exceeds the sum of the resources which it has sold in that year (commodity exports; sale of services abroad; sale of American stock or paper, etc.). The difference must then be balanced by the liquidation of a part of the country's reserves (gold and foreign currencies). The balance of payments of the United States has been in deficit since the mid-1950s. As a consequence, the country's gold reserves fell from $22.8 billion in 1950 to $20.6 billion in 1958, then to $13.2 billion in 1966 and to less than $12 billion at present.

When the origins of this deficit in the U. S. balance of payments are examined, one finds the following:

1) The trade balance is largely in surplus: the United States continues to export many more commodities than are imported.

2) Private capital movements are in balance: net American capital exports equal the net repatriation of profits on capital already invested abroad.

3) The source of the deficit then lies exclusively in: a) governmental aid to foreign countries, that is, the cost of maintaining the imperialist alliances; b) the expenses of the American armed forces abroad, that is, the maintenance of military bases and the conduct of military operations abroad.

It would not be wrong to say that the *increased* deficit in the U. S. balance of payments in 1967 is due three-fourths to the Vietnam war. It should be added, however, that for the past twelve years this deficit takes in the expenses of NATO, SEATO, the operations of the Sixth and Seventh fleets, the landings in Lebanon and Santo Domingo, the antiguerrilla operations in Latin America and Africa, the aid to the military dictatorship in Indonesia, the cost of maintaining the bloody puppet regimes in Taipei, Seoul, and Saigon — all operations prior to or concurrent with the Vietnam war in the strict sense.

Could the gold drain experienced by the United States for more than a decade bring on the "downfall" of the dollar and would this "downfall" threaten the American economy? Let me note first of all that the most powerful capitalists have long had little fear of devaluations of their own currencies. The dollar was devalued on the heels of the economic crisis of 1929-32; that did not reduce but rather increased the profits of the capitalist monopolies. A devaluation of the dollar would not be an economic catastrophe for the United States. It would hit primarily the small foreign and American savers who keep their accumulations in bank deposits or in loans payable in dollars. It could hit the American workers inasmuch as it provokes price rises not compensated for by wage rises. But the American economy would be scarcely shaken by it. On the contrary, a devaluation of the dollar would reduce the prices of American products abroad and increase U. S. exports. In fact, influential bourgeois economists like Paul Samuelson have continually advocated this.

If, nevertheless, the leaders of American capitalism have not taken this road — at least for the present — it is primarily for two reasons. They are afraid of the loss of prestige caused by such a devaluation (or revaluation of the price of gold, which comes to the same thing). They want to prevent the big holders of gold (their West European competitors and the Soviet Union) from gaining by the stroke of a pen the ability to buy 20, 30, or 50 percent more dollars (or American commodities or stocks) with the same amount of gold.

But if the dollar is not devalued for the time being and if the efforts of the Johnson administration do not halt the gold drain but at most succeed in slowing it down, will the United States be in danger of sliding toward bankruptcy? No. If the United States continues to lose its gold it can take three successive measures: abolish the 25 percent gold cover (which is purely formal) for the American banknotes in circulation; forbid the export of gold; demonetize gold — that is, refuse to accept gold in payment for any service or commodity purchased abroad and throw the whole gold stock of the U. S. on the market to penalize the speculators, the Soviet Union, and the European central banks by causing a drop in the price of gold.

Some reply that there are more dollar claims in the hands of foreigners than there is gold in the United States and that such a demonetization of gold would provoke a rise rather than a drop in the price of the precious metal. This objection is not valid. The calculation takes into account only *short-term claims* (which do exceed the U. S. gold stock by 200 percent). It disregards the amount of *foreign stocks and paper* in the hands of U. S. citizens, which is more than double these dollar claims. The United States is in debt to the rest of the world in the short term; the rest of the world is heavily in debt to the United States in the long term. If there were an across-the-board liquidation of debts, not only the Europeans, Japanese, etc., would demand payment in gold or currency for their "treasury notes" payable in dollars; American concerns would also sell their stock in European or Japanese companies and demand payment in dollars. This across-the-board exchange would result in a large deficit for Europe and not for the United States.

To put it differently: one of the sources of the present monetary crisis lies in the fact that the European capitalists are putting their short-term reserves in dollars, while the American capitalists are investing their long-term reserves in Europe. In the long run, this system naturally benefits the Americans. To claim that it shows the "weakness" of the dollar is obviously nonsense.

If this is so, then why do the Americans worry so much about the persistent deficit in their balance of payments? Not because this deficit directly threatens their economy but because it threatens the functioning of the entire international monetary system and thus the *expansion of world trade*. And if the expansion of world trade is halted, American exports will eventually decline in their turn and the entire world economy will be in danger of being drawn into a real deflationary avalanche like 1929.

But precisely because this is American imperialism's principal fear, it stubbornly rejects the return to the gold standard demanded by de Gaulle and his "mentor," Professor Rueff. This cure is worse than the sickness. It entails automatic monetary adjustment which would force the American government to practice a policy of deflation when recessions coincide with balance-of-payments deficits. But to practice a deflationary policy at such times means provoking an economic crisis of exceptional gravity as the Bruening[3] government learned in Germany.

The American capitalists want a flexible money which can be used as a tool for fighting crises. That rules out a return to the gold standard. However, this means that ways must be sought to enlarge the "international liquidity system" by means of a "world money" such as the "right to print money" created by the International Monetary Fund.

The "dollar crisis" and the search for means of international payment independent both of gold and "currency reserves" (dollars and pounds sterling) reflect clear recognition on the part of big international capital of a contradiction inherent in the present-day capitalist system: the contradiction between the dollar's role as an "international money," and its role as an instrument to assure the expansion of the American capitalist economy. To fulfill the first function, a stable money is needed. To fulfill the second function, a flexible money is necessary, i.e., an unstable one. There's the rub.

The dollar's real weakness lies not in the U. S. balance-of-payments deficit. It might even be claimed paradoxically that this deficit reflects the strength rather than the weakness of the American economy. The real weakness of the dollar rests in the enormous governmental and private indebtedness in the United States, without which the formidable American productive machine could no longer sell its flood of commodities. The American private debt went from $140 billion in 1945 to $753 billion in 1963. It came to 78 percent of U. S. gross private production in 1945; it went to 143 percent of this in 1963. In 1951 the average American paid out 14 percent of his disposable income on debts and interest. This now reaches almost 25 percent!

It is clear that this debt spiral, which is a genuine inflationary spiral, cannot continue indefinitely without threatening the underpinnings of the system. A devaluation of the dollar would clearly have the benefit of disadvantaging the creditors and favoring the debtors. But these creditors are the banks and a few big American monopolies; it is understandable that the system hesitates to apply this drastic remedy.

The dollar's weakness thus reflects a weakness inherent in the capitalist system at the present time. The amortization of crises of overproduction through recessions has meant the emergence both of an ever greater surplus productive capacity and a more and more pronounced depreciation of money. Thus we again come to the old Marxist contradiction between the tendency of capital to expand the productive forces in an unlimited manner and the limitations which this same capital imposes on the expansion of the buying power of the "ultimate consumers."

And in the long run, there is no solution to this contradiction—not devaluation of the dollar nor return to the gold standard nor the creation of an "international money." The only solution is abolition of the capitalist mode of production itself.

The Dollar Crisis II

From the April 12, 1968, issue of World Outlook.

Will the dollar follow the pound? Many capitalists both big and little asked themselves this question worriedly in the aftermath of the English devaluation. A couple of weeks ago this worry turned into panic. As a result there was a run on gold, and the central banks of the main capitalist countries had to do something. They instituted a dual "market" in gold — one market for central banks, in which gold continues to be valued at $35 an ounce; and a private or free market in which its price is to be established by the law of supply and demand.

The apparent parallel between the pound and the dollar should not deceive us, however — the position of American capitalism is fundamentally *different* from that of British capitalism.

In Great Britain, the pound sterling's international function as a reserve currency was *in contradiction* to the country's economic decline. Although British industry no longer plays anything but a secondary role in the world economy, the British bourgeoisie stubbornly insists on hanging onto "the good old pound." Nonetheless, sooner or later the pound will cease to serve as a reserve currency, and the sooner this adjustment is made, the better it will be for the British workers. (Their livelihood has just been brutally cut by $1.2 billion to comply with the demands of the international bankers.)

In the United States, on the other hand, the dollar's international role matches the economic power of American imperialism. If for two decades central banks, private banks, and capitalist enterprises have competed for dollars, it is because these dollars represented and still represent a means of purchasing a practically unlimited range of commodities — both consumer goods and machinery. The dollar's function as a reserve currency corresponds to the balance-of-trade deficits most capitalist countries have with the United States.

If tomorrow the United States had to practice a rigorous

deflationary policy, or had to devalue the dollar, this would again strike panic in the other capitalist countries. They would risk losses in three respects. First their sales to the United States would drop and as a result the economic situation of their countries would take a turn for the worse. Secondly, American exports to Europe and Japan would rise and competition would become increasingly stiff. Finally, the threat of a new dollar shortage would arise and this would precipitate endless difficulties in trade and finance.

What is the source of the sudden lack of confidence in the dollar? It certainly does not lie in American private capital exports, because these are in balance with the repatriation of capital dividends to the United States. "The-Americans-who-are-buying-'our'-factories-with-the-paper-dollars-they-are-sending-us" is a Gaullist myth. In reality, the American monopolies are buying up the European factories with the capital which the European banks advance as loans. And these banks loan them this capital because the American monopolies are richer, more solid, make higher profits, and offer more security than the European monopolies. What must be challenged is the whole logic of the capitalist system, not Wall Street's diabolical use ot the dollar.

The lack of confidence in the dollar has been created by the persistent deficit in the American balance of payments, which arises from *U. S. government expenditures abroad.* Hidden behind this discreet rubric are two dramatic operations: financing the Vietnam war; granting military aid to reactionary and dictatorial regimes in many countries (from the military dictatorship in Indonesia to General Mobutu's military dictatorship in the Congo-Kinshasa and from the regime in Seoul to the one in La Paz). It is these dollars that account for the constant flow of gold from the United States; it is these dollars that created the recent panic. One need only pose this problem to recognize the impasse in which the international bourgeoisie finds itself.

For, these dollars are not being spent for narrowly "American" aims; they are being spent to maintain the whole world imperialist system, which is more and more shaken. The real answer to the gold crisis would be to say: "Americans, dissolve your Atlantic pact, SEATO, and your assistance pact with Japan! Liquidate your overseas bases. Bring your soldiers home."

But the international bourgeoisie does not dare give this answer; first of all, because it would risk rapidly provoking that worldwide dollar shortage I have just spoken about; and, secondly, because it would risk leaving world capitalism defenseless against the rising tide of anticapitalist forces throughout the world.

In urging Washington to reestablish its balance of payments, not by eliminating its unproductive foreign spending but by balancing the budget in the United States, the international bourgeoisie would like to force the American workers to pay the full cost of the Vietnam war. Washington, however, is not particularly entranced by this idea, because the opposition to the Vietnam war is already very great. It would like to prevent this opposition from spreading too much among the working class. So, the American answer was, "Pay part yourselves." And the agreement on a dual market in gold does, in fact, imply that the European capitalists will pay part of the costs of this dirty war.

The dual market is only a temporary measure. The free market is precipitating a rise in the price of gold. It is hoped that this increase will bring gold back on the market held in the form of savings (more than a billion dollars a year over the last years). In this way the price would become stabilized and another panic would be avoided.

But two conditions are necessary for this system to function perfectly. First of all, it is necessary that the two markets be completely separate, that is, that no central bank buy gold at $35 an ounce in Washington for resale later at $40 an ounce (or tomorrow at still higher prices) on the free market. But for many small poor countries the temptation is sure to prove too much. Thus there will be lapses. Let us not forget either that American monopolies control some of these countries. For these monopolies, patriotism does not exist, no profits are too small to be overlooked: and they can make sure and substantial profits by trafficking in gold.

Secondly those holding gold must be sure that the American government will not, despite everything, jump the price to $50 or even more. As long as they retain this hope, gold will not be released. And as long as it is not released the price on the free market will threaten to rise apace—that is, speculation will continue and the pressure for devaluing the dollar will grow.

The Americans can "break" the price on the free market by throwing on it a great quantity of gold, that is, by officially demonetizing gold. But they hesitate to take such a step in the absence of complete solidarity among the central banks of all the imperialist powers. Such solidarity is chimerical, however, in the capitalist system, where competition reigns. In these conditions, the plans to create a world currency detached from gold have slight chance of success. This means that the monetary crisis will persist, or more precisely that it will last as long as the capitalist system endures.

The International Monetary Crisis

The following is Chapter Eight of Europe vs. America, *originally published in German in 1968.*[4]

For many years the French government tried to use the chronic deficit in the American balance of payments to reduce America's control of the world's economy and, above all, the power of her corporations in the European market.[5]

This chronic deficit is not the consequence of a deficit in trade; on the contrary, for the last six years there has always been a trading surplus which has fluctuated between four and seven billion dollars a year. The real reasons for the balance of payments deficit should be sought in the export of private capital and, to an even more decisive extent, in overseas military expenditures and "aid" to foreign governments.[6]

French economic theorists of Professor Jacques Rueff's school believe that the chronic deficit in the American balance of payments is nothing but an expression of the "permanent inflation" of the American economy. As long as the international monetary system is based on the gold exchange standard, they consider that the USA is able to afford to buy up foreign companies by means of the excess purchasing power which it has itself created at home. Export of these inflationary dollars furthermore stimulates inflation on a world scale. It increases the dollar reserves of the central banks, who both issue additional national paper currency on the basis of these dollar holdings, and promptly return the dollars to New York and London where they earn short-term interest, thus augmenting the amount of money and credit both in these countries and in America and Britain. This inflationary vicious circle, together with the risk of a sudden withdrawal of capital invested on short term abroad, threatens to throw us back into an economic crisis like that of 1929-33, so they maintain. Rueff's school, and the Gaullist regime influenced by it, saw only one remedy: a return to the gold standard, which would automatically reestablish the American balance of pay-

45

ments, but would also compel American big capital to give up
some of the positions it has occupied in Western Europe. [7]
Without doubt, it is in the field of gold and currency reserves
that one comes closest to finding a reflection of the loss of
the absolute superiority of the USA. In 1938, the USA already had 60 percent of the world's gold reserves. At the end
of the second world war, that proportion had risen to 75 percent. In 1950, it had fallen to 50 percent. In that year, the
USA had a reserve of $22.8 billion, the EEC [European Eco-
nomic Community—Common Market] countries only $3 bil-
lion, and Great Britain $3.7 billion. By 1958, the American
reserves had fallen to $21.4 billion. By 1967, the situation had
been completely reversed. American reserves were only $14.3
billion while those of the EEC countries had climbed to $24.4
billion. By September 1968, American reserves had risen a
little to $14.6 billion and those of the EEC, due to French
losses, had fallen slightly to $23.5 billion. To this should be
added the fact that between 1950 and 1958 U. S. reserves
consisted of gold alone and that today they are only 70 percent gold. The position in the EEC countries has reversed.
The share of gold in their reserves rose from 57 percent in
1958 to 75 percent at the end of 1968. [8] As for monetary
gold, Europe held $15 billion worth in December 1968 against
the USA's $10.5 billion.

The Gaullist government's repeated attacks on dollar inflation and its flat refusal to support the cost of this inflation by
extending the channels of international liquidity created the
mounting tension in the International Monetary Fund, where
Britain and America were calling for broader means of international payment. For many years it has been plain that
international monetary reserves have increased much more
slowly than international trade. According to those in favor of
a return to the gold standard, the slow rate of increase in gold
production—the consequences of a gold price set too low—is
the cause of the trouble. [9] The British and Americans retort that
the trouble is due to an excessively narrow dependence on
gold and to a lack of alternative methods of international
payment. The reserves of all the central banks, together with
the reserves of the International Monetary Fund, were equivalent to 56 percent of the value of world imports in 1956. By
1966 that figure had fallen to 33 percent. Even if the United
States is excluded on the grounds that it is a special case, there
is still a drop from 41 percent to 30 percent.

France, recently supported by the other members of the EEC,
has argued that it would not be enough to create alternative

means of international liquidity so long as the chronic deficit in the American (and British) balance of payments was not made good, for this would only entail the risk of perpetuating and promoting the inflation of the dollar and the pound. When the partisans of a return to the gold standard are shown the dangerous shortage of international means of payment, they usually retort that revaluation of gold by 50 or 100 percent would solve the problem for many decades to come. It is futile to point out to them that such revaluation would principally benefit Western Europe which has more gold than the USA ($10-15 billion worth at the end of 1968) and that it also entirely ignores the liquidity problems of underdeveloped countries.

Increasing tension within the International Monetary Fund has increased the danger of a return to monetary anarchy which would certainly foment a return to monetary nationalism. Antagonized by the pinpricks and the barely disguised attacks of French capital, American big capital has threatened severe retaliation. If the wave of speculation against the dollar were to continue or increase, the USA could engage in a series of measures. First, it could contract the dollar out of its gold warranty (which in fact was done in March 1968); second, it could put an embargo on all gold shipments from the USA; and finally, it could demonetize gold. According to Henry S. Reuss of the American congressional committee on international financial affairs, this would bring the price of gold tumbling down from $35 an ounce to $6. [10] In present circumstances, this would very quickly lead to a dollar shortage in the rest of the world. Such a shortage, after being the chief cause of the difficulties of world capitalism in the first years after the war, was thereafter corrected by a U. S. balance of payments deficit.

The Americans believe that the stability of the dollar is not based on their gold reserves but on the colossal productive capacity of the American economy, and the huge volume of commodities thrown annually on the market at home and abroad. The response to such a line of argument and the answer to a unilateral American embargo on gold shipments would be controls on the import of American capital and goods into Europe. This could only produce a return to intense American protectionism whose disastrous results would be the rapid shrinking of international trade and a general depression.

The hypothesis of a full and complete return to the gold standard only strengthens these conclusions. Between 1929 and 1933, the capitalist economy gave a tragic demonstration of how an unfavorable economic situation coupled with a negative balance of payments compels governments who remain on the gold standard to deflate, to restrain credit and overall demand, instead of pursuing a policy of monetary expansion to stimulate economic recovery. The upshot is inexorable; instead of a mild recession there is a severe economic crisis. Those members of Rueff's school who wish to return to the self-regulating mechanism of gold, want, in fact, to roll history back to the era before Keynes.

This is not the place to expose all the fallacies of "the return to the gold standard" argument. We want to mention only some of the most glaring contradictions.

Rueff and his supporters state that in an economy based on the gold standard, any loss of gold leads to a decrease in effective demand, leading to a fall in prices which automatically stimulates exports, corrects the balance of payments, and raises the level of employment. They forget, first, that when demand falls off in the domestic market, the utilization ratio of productive capacity starts to fall as well, which in monopoly capitalist conditions often provokes not a decrease but an increase in prices, including the prices of key export goods, since big business is keen to maintain its level of profitability (Wilson's deflation in 1966-67 provides a typical example). Second, they leave out the fact that price is not the only criterion of exportability, that there are fluctuations in the demand for export products and in the nature and variety of exports. Third, they forget that fluctuations in foreign demand also affect export possibilities. So when many countries simultaneously experience a decline in employment levels and effective demand, no deflationary measures, no matter how severe, can stimulate exports. The partisans of the gold standard talk as though only monetary crises occur and never crises of overproduction. They overlook the fact that between 1815 and 1914, despite the gold standard general to the West, there were many economic crises some of which were very severe. [11]

No one would deny that for many years the United States has been undergoing a typical state of permanent inflation, but it is also true that the huge American industrial machine can only sell a sufficient amount of its output thanks to the enormous debts of the state, companies, and private citizens [12] which are continuously growing. Any attempt to return to financial orthodoxy would lead at a minimum to stagnation and possibly to a chain of recessions. If we were to return to the gold standard, these recessions would certainly lead to a severe economic slump. [13] In the present situation, American big capital must avoid such an outcome at all costs, for obvious political, social, and military reasons. Consequently a return to the gold standard, dear though it may have been to the Gaullist regime, is pure fantasy.

There can be no doubt that ultimately the extension of public and private indebtedness in the United States, accompanied by a permanent drop in the purchasing power of the dollar, can only lead to considerable economic disorder which is bound to affect the international monetary and commercial system. Modern capitalism is beset by the inherent and objective contradiction between the dollar's role in upholding the level of economic activity inside the USA and its role as the principal instrument of international payments. But as it would not be very rational to precipitate a crisis in the next two or three years to avoid a storm due in fifteen years' time, the American upper bourgeoisie will make no attempt to resolve this contradiction by abandoning its anti-crisis monetary policy (i.e., inflation). The Gaullist solution was equally irrational in so far as an acute American economic crisis would have disastrous consequences on the European capitalist economy. This is further evidence of how wrong it would be to assume that because the American economy has lost its *absolute* superiority it has also lost its *relative* dominance. The American economy is, and will remain for a long time, the most important component of the international capitalist system; to shake it means to shake the whole system. In so far as it was not pure blackmail, Gaullist policy was only an objective indication that certain sectors of the French upper bourgeoisie wanted to saw off the branch on which they were sitting. [14]

We already have one example which shows the consequences of bringing too much pressure to bear on the American economy to reduce the deficit in its balance of payments, and it hardly speaks in favor of the Gaullist thesis. One of the significant components of the deficit in the balance of payments is, as has already been said, the export of capital by the great American monopolies. At present, the American government is counseling these corporations to exercise restraint; but to invest all their accumulated capital profitably, they are compelled to invest part of it in Europe. The ideal solution of this difficulty for American companies is to raise the capital to cover their needs on the European market. In other words, European banks lend American companies the capital which enables them either to deprive European firms of some of their outlets or even simply to buy them up. The European bankers do not do this because they are pro-American but only because

American big business can offer them better securities, higher rates of interest, and wider profit margins. [15]

In the 1966 report of the International Monetary Fund, the total value of money invested by American subsidiaries in Europe between 1962 and 1966 was estimated to be $22.5 billion, only a quarter of which — $5.8 billion — came directly from the USA. The figures show that the role of dollars (that "depreciated paper currency") in buying up "our businesses" has been grossly exaggerated. The international inflationary influence of the dollar and pound holdings of the European central banks (a key argument of the Rueff school) has similarly been exaggerated. Professor Robert Mosse has shown that between 1958 and 1965 the sum total of these holdings which had been reinvested in New York or London had increased by less than $4 billion, a minute fraction of the total amount of money circulating in the USA. [16] It is ridiculous to suggest that such a small sum could be the cause of widespread universal inflation in the world capitalist economy.

The volume of Eurobonds issued (mainly from Luxembourg) climbed rapidly from less than $400 million in 1965 to almost $2 billion in 1967. To these direct issues must be added the significant amount of bank credit extended to the branches of American firms in West Europe. These loans are estimated at a billion dollars for the year 1965. [17] They are supposed to have reached a similar level in 1966 and 1967. This means that in two years, 1965 and 1966, American businesses have raised nearly $7.5 billion on the European capital market. It is unnecessary to explain in detail how this skimming of the West European capital market has undoubtedly strengthened the tendency of the interest rates to climb and industrial profit rates to fall, and contributed to the growing shortage on the capital market and to the present recession which continues in most of the West European countries. Other measures taken by the American central bank network in the last few years to reduce the deficit in the balance of payments have had a similar influence on the situation in Western Europe. [18]

The controversy over the international monetary system between Britain and the USA on the one hand and France (increasingly supported by the whole EEC) on the other is not purely academic, but has more and more implications for the evolution of the economic conjuncture, international as well as European. The growing fear among experts, which was given such pointed expression by the president of the

World Bank at its last session, is not unfounded. The scarcity of international currencies and capital, linked to each other on an international scale, could lead to a sudden plunge in the growth rate of world trade and a speedy end to the international boom.[19]

The most far-sighted European capitalists recognize that their interests are similar to those of American capital in this respect, and that these interests demand an extension of the means of international payment, including the development of a world currency ("paper gold"). This would improve the state of international liquidity quite independently of the role of sterling or the dollar. Robert Triffin's [20] proposal to set up "a central bank of central banks" would have the same effect. It would circulate "central bank certificates."

All such proposals are no more than the expression of the basic fact that the objective socialization of production and international communication is so far advanced that it cries out for a world currency independent of gold. But how can such "world paper money" exist in an economy based on private property? That is to say, on competition based on each firm's private search for profits, on the compulsion to private capital accumulation, leading inevitably to trade cycles and erratic investments. This is the contradiction the system is unable to solve. Besides, such a world currency would only postpone the problem of "secular inflation"; it would not solve it. In the long run it could even make it more explosive.

In any event, a social system which no one can be sure will last into the twenty-first century can obviously not afford the luxury of making long-term plans and considerations the main criteria of its immediate actions. Like the nobility before the French Revolution, whom it resembles in more than one respect, its motto is "Apres nous le deluge!" [After us the deluge!]

The Crisis of the French Franc

From the December 9, 1968, issue of Intercontinental Press.

Three storms in three years' time, that is what the barometer of the international monetary system reveals. There was the devaluation of the pound in November 1967, the dollar crisis in March 1968, and now we have the crisis of the French franc, which threatens to extend to all the European currencies, except the deutsche mark [DM] (and secondarily the Swiss franc and the Dutch florin). Even the dollar is threatened. The future of the system created at Bretton Woods is more than somber. This system is sick. It has entered into its death agony. This death agony may be long, and it takes no Cassandra to predict that the longer its death agony is, the more excruciating it will be.

The bourgeois commentators single out — each according to his taste — as the chief cause of the crisis either the May events in France, speculation, floating capital, or "hot money." They overlook the main item — the worldwide crisis which is inexorably undermining the buying power of *all* the capitalist currencies. The capitalist world could escape this inflation on only two conditions. It must either stop spending for arms and wars or accept the risk of an economic crisis of the 1929 type. Capitalism cannot accept either of these two conditions. If they were accepted, it would only mean that the international bourgeoisie had chosen a quick death over prolonged suffering. Thus, inflation will persist and with it the crisis of the international monetary system.

Doubtless a temporary resuscitation is possible. The expedients proposed to achieve this are well known — raising the price of gold; creating a "central bank currency"; pooling all the exchange reserves of the West European countries (beginning with the reserves of the Common Market countries) in a "Eurofranc" (with or without fusion with the pound) which would serve as a new international reserve currency. The latter presupposes a new stage in the economic unification of capitalist Europe, a decisive advance, because a common currency entails a common government, that is, a common state. The technicians have no lack of choices.

All these solutions are theoretically possible in the context of the international capitalist economy. None of them would undermine the foundations of the capitalist mode of production. But each of them entails considerable sacrifices for sections of the world bourgeoisie, in some cases the sacrifice of interests and immediate profits, in some the sacrifice of sovereignty, and in some political prestige and power. This means that the new world monetary conference which the Nixon administration will doubtless call next year seems fated to be difficult and that even these expedients will not be easy to apply.

None of these expedients, however, cease to be what they are—devices to gain time, to postpone a new monetary crisis without dealing even remotely with the fundamental cause. I wrote seven years ago that neocapitalism is caught in a vise from which it cannot escape. International exchanges and payments—on which capitalist "prosperity" is increasingly dependent—require a stable currency. But a policy aimed against crises, recessions, and business cycles requires a flexible currency. The one goal cannot be obtained without sacrificing the other.

Thus the successive tempests which have shaken all these currencies prove that "modern," "technocratic," "managed" capitalism has by no means succeeded in overcoming its fundamental contradictions. The defeat of the pound, the franc, and the dollar is a triumph for Karl Marx, that is, a blatant demonstration of the incurable sickness of the capitalist system. The ability to sell 200 million television sets and 100 million cars, thanks to constant inflation of the volume of money, may have suggested that prosperity had become permanent. The crisis of the capitalist currencies is a harsh reminder of the reality. This "prosperity" is a house of cards that can be toppled by any gust of wind.

Luck would have it that it is Schiller's [21] turn to be the minister presiding over the "Club of the Ten," which includes the ten major imperialist powers of the world. The club meeting called to decide the fate of French finances was therefore held in Berlin. Chance is often responsible for many things. It made possible a spectacular demonstration of the change in the relationship of forces in capitalist Europe which had actually already occurred years ago. As the November 28, 1968, London *Times* observed with both realism and a certain bitterness, this crisis may represent the turning point in the development of power relationships in Europe. The German Federal Republic has emerged as the main power of capitalist Europe.

I also predicted this at the time de Gaulle precipitated the first crisis in the Common Market. The only possible counterweight against the West German bourgeoisie's clear superiority in capitalist Europe would be the entry of Great Britain into the Common Market and the acceleration of the trend toward the interpenetration of capital in Europe. There would have been no West German hegemony in the giant multinational companies owned by the German, British, French, Italian, Benelux, Swiss, and Swedish capitalists. When de Gaulle blocked Great Britain's entry into the Common Market and tried to defend "French sovereignty" over the factories in France, the German drive for hegemony became irresistible. The general was working for the king of Prussia. [22]

The origin of this hegemony and its limits must be understood. In Eastern Europe they like to consider Bonn as "the No. 1 United States satellite in Europe," or at least Washington's "most favored ally." This is an oversimplification of a much more complex relationship. It is true that the West German bourgeoisie, deprived of all real military power, could reconstruct its industrial power only under the Pentagon's nuclear umbrella. But it is still more true that its revival expresses economic realities independent of all foreign aid — an industrial production far exceeding that of any other European power, an export boom, a technological level and advance toward automation ahead of the rest of the continent.

Even more can be said. Bonn's industrial and financial expansion — the solidity of the deutsche mark is the result of an enormous excess of exports over imports which expresses a competitive power unrivaled in Europe or in the world — today frightens American imperialism. It frightens the American imperialists to such an extent that they have been concentrating all their efforts on getting a revaluation of the DM, which would limit German exports, beginning with those to the USA (in the first six months of 1968, these increased 48 percent over the corresponding period in the previous year!). Schiller's "no" was not so much a "no" to de Gaulle or Wilson. It was a "no" to Washington. At that moment something fundamental changed, not only in the relationship of forces in Europe, but in the relationship of forces between Germany and the United States.

Since Bonn refused to revalue the DM, de Gaulle was confronted with a clear ultimatum — either devalue the French franc or apply a severe austerity policy. The "Ten" forced this choice on him, the same way they imposed the "incomes policy" on Wilson last year. If he had not done one of these two things, he would not have gotten the three billion dollars in credit which would make it possible to stop up the breach opened by speculation. He delighted Washington and London by choosing austerity instead of devaluation. Any new devaluation would have immediately undermined the stability of the pound and subjected even the dollar to a harsh test.

The policy of the imperialist powers today is a dialectical unity of two opposites — interimperialist competition and imperialist solidarity against common enemies and dangers. In November as in May, the feeling that "we are all in the same boat" quickly took the place of Schadenfreude [enjoying the misery of others]. They were very happy to see de Gaulle's prestige seriously damaged, but a collapse of the French currency threatened to rock the entire international monetary system. Still, within the framework of the solidarity, which played the fundamental role, competition did not lose its claims. The main center of decision-making in Europe moved from Paris to Bonn.

The next move is up to the German bourgeoisie. They can play it in one of two ways. They can give immediate economic interests priority or they can favor their long-range political interests. The first orientation would mean giving fresh impetus to the Common Market, putting pressure on de Gaulle to drop his veto of Great Britain's entry, accelerating the interpenetration of European capital, creating a common European currency. The second orientation would mean giving priority to the establishment of a "European striking force," that is, secure the access to nuclear weapons which the West German bourgeoisie have coveted for fifteen years. This would bring the military relationship of forces into line with the relationship of economic forces. It would at the same time open up an international crisis of extreme gravity in Europe, because it is unlikely that the Soviet Union would stand by passively in the face of the nuclear rearmament of the principal capitalist power on the continent.

From the technical standpoint, the cause of the crisis of the franc was different from the cause of the downfall of the pound. The latter was precipitated by a chronic deficit in the balance of payments, the expression of the structural crisis of British imperialism. The cause of the crisis of the franc was a speculative flight of capital which in the space of a few months drained away almost half of France's exchange reserves.

However, all those, from de Gaulle to Fowler, the American

secretary of the treasury, who say that the French economic situation remains "fundamentally sound" pass over an essential aspect of the franc crisis. In order to absorb the revolutionary crisis of May-June 1968, the French bosses and government had to concede wage increases which raised labor costs by 15 percent and cost prices by at least 5 percent. French industry's competitive capacity, already reduced as a result of German (and in some sectors Italian) technological superiority, and damaged by the devaluation of the pound, was struck another blow. French imports already exceed exports by 6 percent. The more rapid rise in prices in France than in Germany, Great Britain, or Italy, could only accentuate this disequilibrium. The speculators, by *anticipating* a future gold and currency drain caused by a worsening of the balance-of-payments deficit, obviously precipitated this development. But they did not cause it. It was inherent in the logic of the Grenelle agreements. [23]

The Gaullist economic policy has now been stamped with the seal of total incoherence. Logically there are two alternatives for absorbing the rise in production costs — expansion, that is a rapid increase in productivity (it has been estimated that almost 30 percent of productive capacity was unutilized on the eve of the revolutionary upsurge of May 1968!); or devaluation, that is, restoring competitiveness, compensating for increased costs in francs by cutting the cost of the franc in terms of foreign currency. The Couve de Murville cabinet has constantly vacillated between expansion and deflation.

By playing the deflationary card now — because that is what austerity comes down to! — it is accelerating the rising cost of living still more (in the guise of the charges for public services) while slowing the increase in productivity (by reducing investment, the rate of utilization of the productive apparatus, or even aggregate demand, if unemployment rises rapidly). Thus, it is making inroads into the competitiveness of French industry on both sides. Export subsidies will not change much in this regard unless imports are taxed at the same time to a point that would break up the whole Common Market.

But this *economic* incoherence has a striking *social* meaning. In the grip of the "great fear" of May, when socialist revolution was beating at the door, the French bourgeoisie wanted to save the essential thing, that is, its class power. It rallied behind its supreme savior and was ready to pay the bill. But once the fear receded, they became their old selves again. De Gaulle had the outlandish idea of levying some small taxes on large incomes and inheritances in order to limit inflation. Immediately a mutiny broke out. What a "psychological blunder"! What "an Invitation to the Waltz," that is, to a flight of capital! Putting a knife to the throat of the French government, in a couple of visits to the Zurich and Frankfurt banks, big capital forced it to change its economic and social policy from top to bottom. The workers themselves will pay the bill for May. The wage earners will take the beating instead of the speculators. That is the logic of the capitalist system.

Now all these nice people are unmasked and the spectacle is not exactly an attractive one. Patriotism is good for sending soldiers to be killed, or, in a pinch, for stampeding the electorate. But above all, don't let anybody ask us to sacrifice our hoards in the interest of the country. When it is a question of winning or losing 10 percent, the national borders disappear.

The general's nationalist rhetoric is good for naive television viewers or for Andre Malraux's anthologies. But when the speculators crack the whip, de Gaulle cringes like any undersecretary of state of the Fourth Republic. Put revolutionary students in prison, right away! But neither prison nor confiscation will touch the profits — to say nothing of the fortunes — of big capital which is trying to bring down the franc. They prefer to freeze wages. That is obviously easier.

What a comedown, what a revolting comedy! But also what an object lesson for 10 million French workers. In May they had power within their grasp. On the advice of misleaders, they let it go in exchange for two illusions — the illusion of parliamentary elections, which in an imperialist "democracy" cannot help but be manipulated; and the illusion of wage increases, which big capital can absorb rapidly by price and tax increases. This will no doubt be completed by the beginning of 1969.

It is true that the patriotic refrain is already being heard again. And, in the wake of a three-billion-dollar capital flight organized by the French bourgeoisie, a paper like *Le Monde* [24] was not ashamed to write: "The French people are no less all in the same boat." (November 26, 1968.)

Are they really in the same boat? Will the costs be distributed "equitably" after an "equitable" distribution of the profits? Where is the tax on capital which would confiscate all the profits of the speculators? Where is the opening of the books and the elimination of banking secrecy which would make it possible to track down all these profits and show that a part of the capital sent abroad was made up of state credits accorded to businesses? Where is the workers' control which would deprive the employer-speculators of the power to impose their will like a divine right on the workers in the plants when they have lost all moral credit?

This is what the workers will remember at the March meeting,[25] when the accounting will have to be made. This is what must arouse them to an energetic defense of their June 1968 economic gains. This above all is what must arouse them to aim higher than their trade union leaders did in May and June— to set their sights on power in the plants and power in the state, without which no gain can be consolidated. In taking the option of a frontal attack against the jobs and wages of the workers, de Gaulle has ensured a singular hastening of the next social explosion in France.

The Devaluation of the French Franc

From the September 8, 1969, issue of Intercontinental Press.
Originally published in the August 16, 1969, issue of the Belgian revolutionary-socialist weekly La Gauche. *Translated by* Intercontinental Press. *Written in response to the 12.5 percent devaluation of the French franc on August 11, 1969.*

De Gaulle leaves — and now comes the devaluation of the French franc. Clearly, the long-range effects of the May 1968 revolutionary upsurge are far from over.

At the time of the alarm over possible devaluation of the franc in November 1968, I indicated the concatenation that would make this move inevitable. The across-the-board wage increase which the bourgeoisie was forced to grant in May to avert a revolution could not help but slow down exports and increase imports. A balance of payments deficit inevitably flowed from this, a hemorrhaging of exchange reserves. The losses incurred by the Bank of France since the beginning of 1969 total more than $600 million. In the month of July alone, it lost $138 million. All this made devaluation inevitable.

I wrote last November that while the speculators precipitated the crisis of the franc, they did not cause it. They merely accelerated the crisis by anticipating the actual development.

Today everyone admits that the permanent balance of payments deficit since May was the real cause of the fall of the franc. But the capitalist system is so constructed that speculators are always rewarded. On August 11, small savers lost 12.5 percent of the value of their savings as measured in gold or foreign currency. They will soon lose the same amount in buying power as a result of a rise in prices. On the other hand, all the speculators who placed their capital abroad retain the full value of their assets. By repatriating a part of this capital before the price rise reaches 12.5 percent, their buying power will have increased. An injustice? Obviously. But isn't the capitalist system based on inequality, that is, basic injustice in the relations between capital and labor, between the rich and the poor?

The injustice obviously does not stop there. For the workers, the devaluation offers nothing but rising prices. The results for them are negative up and down the line. The industrialists, businessmen, and property owners will find their assets immediately revalued. Even before the price spiral begins, the prices of land, real estate, jewels, and securities (starting with foreign stocks and bonds) are moving into line with the prices of gold, the dollar, and the deutsche mark.

Next, businessmen and industrialists will try to revalue their predevaluation inventories by selling them or evaluating them in accordance with the new rate. The price through September 15 announced by the French government was aimed at blocking this maneuver. However, its success is not assured in a climate dominated by an inflationary tendency in credit and the means of payment.

Finally, as soon as the French capitalists are compelled to import products at higher costs than previously, they will try to shift this cost onto the French consumers, helping the process along as best they can. When raw materials account for one-third of the cost-price of a product, who is going to prevent a manufacturer or dealer from increasing his sales prices by 5 or 6 percent rather than the 4.17 percent "technically" justified from the capitalist point of view?

The discontent and disquiet of the unions, which merely reflect the general sentiment, are therefore quite understandable. The devaluation represents yet another redistribution of the French national income in favor of capital and at the expense of labor, the latest push by capital to neutralize the concessions granted the workers under threat of revolution in May 1968, if not to reduce the share of labor below the pre-May level.

In this sense, the devaluation was in the logic of things. It illustrated once again the logical implications of the referendum and the presidential election. Contrary to the myth widely held among the respectable left, it was not the workers who forced de Gaulle out of office through the referendum. It was the layer of capitalists represented by Giscard d'Estaing, Pleven, and Duhamel, who felt that the time had come to get rid of a leader who had become an incumbrance, having lost his effectiveness.

Pompidou was elected president of the republic thanks to the support of this section of the bourgeoisie. Now they are presenting their bill — devaluation (that is, rehabilitation of the speculators), a European policy (i.e., orienting toward the internationalization of capital required by the big monopolies);

sustained inflation (i.e., soaking up the last gains the workers made in May). It was not known whether de Gaulle was prepared to carry out this policy rapidly and without reservations. But in the case of Pompidou, there was not the slightest doubt. The play is being enacted in faithful agreement with the text and the intentions of the authors.

But while the immediate succession of events is perfectly logical — that is, it corresponds to the interests of the big French employers — the economic strategy behind the devaluation seems much more dubious. The timing of the operation has been admired. It was carried out during the vacation period when speculation was at its low point (even the interest rate on the Eurodollar market began to weaken in July, something not seen for a long time), while perfect secrecy was maintained. Nonetheless, the success of a devaluation is not measured by the immediate circumstances surrounding it. When we examine the broad economic context, we are led rather to conclude that the measure came much too late and the danger is that most of its effectiveness will be lost.

In order to achieve the desired goal — that is, reestablish an equilibrium in the balance of payments — the devaluation would have to result in an increase in the volume of French sales abroad (above all in the neighbor countries and in the United States) and in a drop in imports. But two series of developing economic changes make these results doubtful. On the one hand, a climate of pronounced inflation prevails in France. The official price index has risen by 3.5 percent since the beginning of the year — that is, at a yearly rate of 6.5 percent — and in reality, prices have risen by almost 5 percent, or at a yearly rate of more than 9 percent. Excess productive capacity is limited. It is not likely, therefore, that a major part of industrial production can be diverted from the domestic market toward foreign markets. The fact that French products will in fact — for the immediate future — be cheaper on the export market will increase foreign demand for these products. This new foreign demand will be added to a demand on the domestic market which is already in excess of supply. The probable result, then, will be an accentuated inflation with only a modest increase in exports.

Moreover, in the United States, the boom has finally been dampened by deflationary measures taken by the government. A downturn is foreshadowed for the next year in West Germany and possibly also in Italy and Great Britain. The price rises in those countries will, then, probably flatten out. At the first downturn, the German exporters are perfectly capable of giving major discounts in order to "hold" their foreign markets. Thus, imports into France threaten to remain as high as they are today. And, despite the devaluation, French products threaten to remain not very competitive—in many branches of industry—with respect to those of most of France's major commercial partners.

The key to success in the operation would have been to devalue the currency while avoiding inflation, or a rise in prices. But this key is more than ever out of the reach of the government of French capitalism.

If we consider the social repercussions, things appear even gloomier for French capitalism. After the squall in November 1968, there was no "March meeting," 25 that is, the new social explosion that was generally expected did not take place. But there have been hundreds of strikes in large and small enterprises. These testify to the combativity of the workers, which has remained intact since May 1968. Furthermore—and this has been unheard of in France for twenty years—now, in the middle of the vacation period, stubborn strikes are going on among the steelworkers in Lorraine and the building-trades workers in Lacq, to cite only two examples.

Under such conditions, the union federations, which have strained every effort to keep strikes since June 1968 from spreading, will have a difficult time in resisting the more and more widespread demands for wage increases to "recover" the gains of May that have been soaked up by inflation and devaluation. From the standpoint of the class struggle, France appears to be in for a "hot" fall and winter.

If social tensions mount, the bosses will again have to dump ballast, because they are even less capable than they were in May 1968 of holding down the lid on a vast popular upsurge. Any new concession to the workers would immediately wipe out the effects of the devaluation and confront the French bosses and bourgeois leaders with the very dilemma that has terrified them since June 1968 and especially since November 1968.

The death agony of the international monetary system can only quicken after the devaluation of the franc. While the speculation we are now witnessing will doubtless not affect the immediate situation, the bankers and capitalists have their eyes fixed on September 29, 1969, when the results will be in for the legislative election in West Germany the preceding day.

It is no secret that the "specialists" in international monetary relations want a general realignment of currencies. The devaluation of the French franc was to be one of the aspects of this realignment, the kingpin of which would be the upward revaluation of the deutsche mark, the Italian lira, and the Japanese yen (opinions are more divided on where to fit in the Dutch florin, the Belgian franc, and the pound sterling).

It is not hard to understand that such a general realignment would be a windfall for the U. S. capitalists, whose principal competitors would thus find themselves forced to sell their commodities at higher prices on the U. S. domestic market.

If Bonn, Rome, and Tokyo turn down this proposal, the United States has a powerful weapon in its arsenal. It can continue its policy of deflation, of boosting interest rates, which would threaten to touch off a generalized recession in the economies of the imperialist countries and would cause them heavier losses than those accruing from the proposed currency revaluations.

We should never lose sight of the fact that monetary crises merely express much more deep-seated capitalist contradictions. And, in face of the threat of a general economic recession which is shaping up on the horizon, we can bet that the directors of the central banks and the ministers of finance of the capitalist countries will do their utmost in their decisions over the coming months to maintain a minimum of cohesiveness — save for yelling "every man for himself!" if the lightning strikes to close.

This, in fact, is the reality of capitalism today, confronted as it is with ever more powerful foes and dangers which threaten its very existence. It cannot help but be continually buffeted between the desire for "international solidarity" and the temptations of "sacrosanct self-interest" which will remain as long as private property exists.

August 12, 1969

Revaluation of the Deutsche Mark

From the October 27, 1969, issue of Intercontinental Press. *Originally appeared in the Belgian weekly* La Gauche *shortly before the 9.3 percent revaluation of the German mark on October 24, 1969. Translated by* Intercontinental Press.

The pressure for an upward revaluation of the deutsche mark has become irresistible. It will come as soon as the changing of the guard in Bonn is confirmed by the Bundestag. 26 What does it mean? What does it reveal? What does it point to?

At first view, the revaluation of the deutsche mark looks like a triumph for American diplomacy. U. S. big capital has applied the most conspicuous pressure for this result, backed up in particular by the City of London. The reason why these two powers favor revaluation of the deutsche mark is hardly mysterious. It would force their most formidable competitor to raise his prices on their principal foreign markets.

A 7 percent revaluation of the deutsche mark would mean that German industrial products would cost 7 percent more in the United States and elsewhere. (This is only true, however, so long as the German exporters do not succeed in "reabsorbing" the costs of the revaluation and the export tax is maintained in the Federal Republic. There may be a disagreeable surprise in store for the Anglo-American industrialists on this score!)

The American capitalists, moreover, would like to see the West German example imitated by other formidable competitors — the Japanese capitalists (the pressure will shift onto them next), or the Italian capitalists. Strongly pinned down by their working class, the Italians will defend themselves with the courage of desperation. The Japanese will most likely have to yield.

From the standpoint of the monetary experts, the triumph of American imperialism looks still more impressive. When one capitalist country has a deficit in its balance of payments (as the United States has) and another a surplus (as Germany has), the "normal" procedure has always been for the deficit country to devalue its currency, and for the gold parity of the currency of the country with a surplus to remain unchanged. Speculation, that is, capital transfers and flights, has been sufficient to achieve this result, as recently in the case of the French franc.

However, in the age of the gold-dollar standard, no speculative movement can force American imperialism to devalue. The United States has decided, for all practical purposes, not to give up any more gold in the "normal manner." The monetary experts have had their breath taken away: "Vice not virtue is being rewarded!" Instead of the dollar being devalued, the deutsche mark is being revalued.

But in making this observation, these same experts, without realizing it, are mixing up appearance and reality. *Because this is exactly what the revaluation of the deutsche mark is— a devaluation of the dollar!*

This will become still clearer should the Japanese yen and other currencies such as the Italian lira and the Dutch florin or the Swiss franc become caught up in the whirlwind of revaluation. But it still holds true even if the revaluation is restricted to the deutsche mark alone.

As soon as things are viewed in this way, the American "triumph" begins to look a lot like a Pyrrhic victory. In the October 7, 1969, issue of *Le Monde*, Paul Fabra proclaimed: "The supremacy of the dollar has become so total that for the first time in perhaps ten years the U. S. balance-of-payments deficit . . . was not even brought up before the general assembly of the International Monetary Fund." By way of conclusion, Fabra added: "Finally, if, in spite of this imposing display, the dollar is not yet [!] 'as good as gold,' it is because it continues to be threatened on the domestic front, that is, by the inflation in America itself. . . ."

This "not yet" is worth its weight in gold. We can bet that the American capitalists are engaging in some bitter reflections on a currency whose "total supremacy" is characterized by an annual loss of 6 percent of its buying power. . . .

In actuality, the inflation in the United States, this loss of buying power, is no mere "domestic" matter. It rebounds against American capitalism throughout the world. It forces the big U. S. corporations, which formerly managed to pay their creditors' interest of 3 to 4 percent a year, to borrow in Europe at rates of 8 percent like any ordinary ministate (Belgium, for instance). This inflation is provoking a general flight from the dollar, not only among the private

capitalists but even among the principal central banks. This
reflects not a "total supremacy," but to the contrary *a loss of
industrial supremacy* which is astounding.

This is explained in part by the fact that owing to the U. S.
refusal to devalue the dollar, the American inflation has had
repercussions on the country's export prices. No one has drawn
attention to this aspect. In the first five months of 1969, West
Germany (whose population is only one-fourth that of the United
States) exported more than a billion dollars worth of goods to
the U. S., which is more than it imported from the U. S. In both
April and May, 1969, Germany's total exports of machines
and transportation equipment exceeded $1.1 billion. At this
rate, these exports would come to $13.2 billion over a year's
period, thus equaling the figure for U. S. exports of producer
goods. A few years ago, exports of American producer goods
to Germany were still 20 percent higher than imports. This
U. S. "triumph" is really impressive.

In interimperialist competition, the battle is decided by competitive capacity, and this, in the last analysis, is a function of
three factors — the volume of capital, the level of productivity,
and the level of wages.

With regard to the first factor, American imperialism enjoys
a comfortable lead; with regard to the second, its lead is being
eaten away year by year; as for the third factor, American
imperialism suffers a considerable handicap. And in this area,
the inflation can only increase the difficulties for the U. S., inasmuch as it compels the American workers to demand more
and more substantial wage increases.

The flight of capital — "international speculation" — is an antici-
patory movement, which obviously can bring the day of reckoning closer. But in the last analysis, it is the development
of competitive capacity which is decisive. During the two weeks
the deutsche mark was offered at a "floating rate," France lost
all the currency reserves it had gained since the devaluation of
the franc.

In this context, the revaluation of the deutsche mark represents an attempt by big capital east of the Rhine to stop a
chain reaction which could mortally threaten the entire international monetary system, that is, capitalist world trade.

When certain capitalist countries enjoy a considerable surplus
in their balance of payments, they cannot help but attract
capital "fleeing" from those countries that have deficits, where
a devaluation seems inevitable sooner or later. But, by themselves, neither revaluation nor devaluation change the situation.
They only change it if the relationship of productive forces

changes, if the competitive capacity of a country suffering a deficit is restored. But such a change is not a function only of exchange rates. It is also a function of relative industrial productivity, of capitalist profit rates (which determine whether or not it is possible to "neutralize" the modification of the exchange rates), of the relationship of forces between the classes.

Although it may seem surprising, since the Social Democrats have been the great advocates of revaluation—is this really so paradoxical?—the revaluation is primarily a psychological operation aimed against the German working class. The government and the bosses will tell the workers and the unions: "See, there is no longer any reason for you to get excited. Inflation has been staved off. The buying power of the deutsche mark is secure. So, be satisfied with 'reasonable' raises. Don't forget that the competitive capacity of German industry has been damaged by the revaluation. If you demand excessive wage raises, exports will drop and we will find ourselves in a recession. Don't kill the goose that lays the golden eggs." This amounts to saying that the German workers must be satisfied with the *reduced* share of the national income that was forced on them as a result of the 1966-67 recession and its consequent unemployment now when there is full employment again.

Will the German workers let themselves be taken for a ride? That is not certain. And last month's strike wave [27] is grounds for hoping that they will not. At any rate, all the speeches about "capital flight" have not prevented the Italian workers from demanding—and getting—quite substantial wage increases.

All this reflects the fact that "overheating" is again developing in the economies of several European countries and that this development will end up in a recession, which, unlike the one in 1966-67, might well coincide with an American recession. It is this prospect that sends cold chills up and down the spines of the Common Market financial experts.

Up until now, the American workers have been the principal victims of this merry-go-round. Their buying power has been declining for several years, while the purchasing power of the European workers, despite everything, has risen markedly. This is the only "positive" aspect of the American inflation for U. S. big capital—it enables it to reduce the disparity between wages in the United States and Europe. But here again the question is whether the American workers will let themselves be had. In 1967 and 1968, the hours of work lost because of strikes in the United States were double the average in the years 1960-66, nearly double that of 1964, 1965, and 1966, and more than double that in 1960, 1961, 1962, and 1963.

The American workers are defending their steaks, and the "wage disparity" remains more or less intact. The only remedy is a new American recession with an increase in unemployment. The Nixon regime is working on this in its own way. But it is a drastic remedy because the United States has become the principal market of all the other imperialist countries, and an American recession would strike all the other capitalist economies, thus reducing their capacity to import American products.

To sum up. The crisis of the international monetary system has not been produced by technical causes. It is not the product of errors made by the governments. It simply reflects the fact that without inflation, American — and international — capitalism can no longer avert serious recessions.

The maneuvers we are witnessing for the moment have a double meaning. Every imperialist class is trying to shift the burden of an adjustment, which has become inevitable, onto the shoulders of the working class of its country and onto the shoulders of its competitors (that is, the workers in the competing countries). The workers will not remain passive in the face of these attempts to create and export unemployment. Immediate self-defense is required. But the best defense is the best offense, that is, challenging a system whose bankruptcy is once again apparent, despite ten years of boasting by its exponents.

The World Economic Situation

The following is a portion of a talk given by Ernest Mandel in December 1969.

The eight-year boom of the American economy is finished. The only question still to be decided is whether the American economy faces a real recession or just stagnation. In Western Europe, the boom is still continuing in several countries, especially the most important one: West Germany. But there are many signs indicating that this is now declining and that a considerable slowdown in economic growth will occur in capitalist Europe, too, in 1970. The overheating of the West German economy makes probable a new West German recession. The key question is whether this West German recession will take place in 1970 or in 1971.

This is a key question because a narrow time lag between the U. S. recession and the West German recession could induce a generalized recession throughout the whole international capitalist economy. On the other hand, if there is a considerable time lag then the differing economic conditions in the main countries of the capitalist world can cushion the depth of the recession each one undergoes.

In addition, a recession in the United States would create new supplementary difficulties for the semicolonial countries. It would touch off a downtrend in the prices of most raw materials, with all the consequences this would signify for the economies of many semicolonial countries.

The only important capitalist country that seems to be able to escape the consequences of this downward movement in 1970 seems to be Japan. There the boom still continues out of domestic resources and out of the consequences of the Vietnam war. Nevertheless, we should not forget that nearly 20 percent of Japanese exports go to the United States; so that a recession in the U. S. could not fail to affect the Japanese economy, too.

Definite signs of an actual recession in the United States

69

have already appeared. For several months, industrial production has dipped. Inventories have built up at a very rapid pace. Total expendable income is increasing more slowly than prices, which means that real income is declining. Orders for investment goods have stopped growing at the same rate as before. Because certain fiscal measures favoring investment are being ended, it is forecast that productive investment will decline. One sector, which is a key sector in the American economy, the automobile industry, has already been seriously hit. In some key automobile factories, a serious reduction in current output is to be seen. Unemployment figures rose significantly as the fall season opened. It is true that unemployment dropped in November, but this was a result of statistical legerdemain. When a recession begins in any capitalist country with a rather high standard of living, one of the first consequences is that a number of people, as the bourgeois economists say, "drop out of the labor market." This means that housewives and young people in particular stop looking for work because they know they won't be hired anyway.

The coinciding of these signs seems to indicate the probability of a recession in the first half of 1970. If I nevertheless advise the comrades to take a cautious attitude, it is essentially because of the following reason: the American capitalist class is still divided as to the seriousness of the danger of inflation and how far to go in ending this danger. There is no doubt that the immediate reason for the current recession is the anti-inflationary measures taken by the government. I say, of course, the "immediate reason," and not the deeper reason. We know that the deeper reasons lie in the classical contradictions of capitalism. But whereas all the bankers and financial authorities of the Nixon administration favor continuing with the anti-inflationary measures, that is to say, making certain that a recession occurs in the U. S. next year, one wing of the capitalist class, particularly the capitalist politicians, favor slowing down these measures. At this very moment, Congress is debating a big tax reduction. If enacted, this would of course increase inflationary purchasing power and the tax reduction would stand in complete contradiction to the general policies of the Nixon administration. The outcome of the debate will be determined partially by the interests of particular politicians who face election contests in 1970 and want to be reelected regardless of the cost to the capitalist economy of the United States as a whole. To grant the concession of a tax reduction is one way of getting reelected, they think.

But behind these very limited sectional interests of the bourgeois politicians there is a more basic difference of opinion
in the capitalist class. This difference of opinion is closely
linked with what we could call the impending intensification of
the class struggle in the United States. The capitalist class has
to make a judgment on the relationship of forces between it
and the working class inside the United States. As we all know
from European experience, a recession is an excellent weapon
against the working class under "normal" capitalist conditions.
It puts pressure on wages, it creates unemployment, divides
the workers, and has a whole series of consequences favorable
to the capitalists in the daily class struggle. A whole wing,
probably the majority, of the American capitalist class is de-
liberately moving in that direction today.

But another wing of this same bourgeoisie is afraid that
a big increase in unemployment would intensify the radicalization of the Black and youthful sectors of the American working
class and would spread the growing radicalization in American
society to sectors of the adult white working class that are still
apathetic politically today. They are apprehensive that the
workers would react even more violently against unemployment
than they have against inflation and the rising cost of living.
This is a real dilemma, because they cannot fight inflation
without creating unemployment, and they cannot avoid unemployment without increasing inflation.

As for the possible effects of an American recession on the European economy, in general most of the capitalist experts in
Europe worry about this, particularly in view of the fact that
in a series of European economies, monetary, financial, economic, or social instability has significantly increased in the
recent period. I think we can place France, Britain, and Italy
in this category today, that is to say, three of the four major
capitalist powers of Europe. And any supplementary cause
of unrest, already alarming to the capitalist class, could of
course very gravely increase the political and social instability
in these countries.

I should like to indicate only one factor in this relation that
is generally underestimated by bourgeois politicians and especially by bourgeois economic experts and that is a direct
result of the long-term inflationary trend. There is something
like $20 billion of European capital floating around in the
American stock market system, a not insignificant part of
which is in the form of stocks of investment trusts, some of
which are operating on a highly speculative and even semi-
crooked basis. This is a very big sum of money for European

capitalism. I'm thinking especially of the so-called real estate investment trusts. Just to give you a point of reference: the total foreign capital investment of all the imperialist powers today is around $100 billion. So this amount alone is one-fifth of the total international capital investment.

If these capitalists become panicked and start to think that a collapse can occur in Wall Street, or that some of these international investment trusts that have been built on the assumption of a constant rise in stock, bond, and land prices might collapse and even go bankrupt, capital will flow out of these schemes and this could have many grave results for international capitalism. I suppose we have no stock market experts in the hall, but some comrades will have read in the newspapers that Wall Street's stock market index, from a max-imum of above 1,000 will probably drop below 700 within the next few days. It is already around 720 and is plunging every day. This means the stock market speculators confront much knottier problems today than the revolutionists.

The American capitalist class has been dealt a very powerful blow by the successful resistance of the Vietnamese revolution. Inside the United States it has been confronted with three suc-cessive waves of mass radicalization: first the radicalization of the Black masses, then the radicalization of the students, and now a mass antiwar movement that has obviously begun to go beyond the limits of a purely student movement. It is clear that in such an atmosphere, the more clear-sighted poli-ticians in the bourgeois camp cannot take lightly the perspective of a supplementary radicalization of the white working class and the opening up, so to speak, of a new home front inside the United States while the Vietnam war is still going on—not only a Black revolt on the home front, and the antiwar move-ment, but increasing tension between the white workers and the capitalists.

I say this because my own conviction is that whatever de-cisions the capitalists may take—and probably they will decide to continue the anti-inflationary measures; that is to say, head towards a recession in 1970—it seems hardly possible that they can view the perspective of five, six, or seven million unem-ployed in the United States lightly. For that reason, I believe that as soon as the recession has reached a certain point, they will revert to anti-recession measures in order to limit unemployment. And we must understand that they still have the resources needed to do this. Such a turn will intensify the contradictions of the world capitalist system. It will deepen the crisis of the world monetary system. It will provoke sharp reactions among the European capitalists. But faced with the danger of an acute social crisis inside the United States, the probability is that "sacred egoism," as the capitalists say, will gain the upper hand over other considerations.

The Open Decline of the Dollar

From the May 24, 1971, issue of Intercontinental Press. *In first week of May 1971, massive dumping of dollars in anticipation of a devaluation had forced the temporary closing of foreign exchange markets in several European countries.*

Nine years ago, I made the following assessment of the international economic situation: "The dilemma confronting the state in the period of capitalist decline is that of *choosing between crisis and inflation.* The former cannot be avoided without accentuating the latter. . . . Monetary stability—which, by definition, is limited in time—thus appears as the insurmountable barrier against which, in the long run, the moderating intervention of the state in the economic cycle is brought up short. The contradiction between the dollar as an anticyclical device in the United States and the dollar as money of account on the world market has already become insurmountable."[28]

This diagnosis has not been contradicted by the events. It indicates a *dilemma* that most of the bourgeois commentators on the present monetary crisis seem not yet to have understood. In fact, the crisis of the international monetary system set up in Bretton Woods at the end of the second world war has become quasi-permanent. The fifth stage of this crisis opened in 1967. But while the first gusts hit the pound sterling and later the French franc—whereas the pressure on the dollar seemed to be eased by the U. S. halt in gold sales—this time the dollar itself has been caught up in the whirlwind. "The dollar standard," which some insisted on condemning as a permanent drain on the riches of capitalist Europe for the benefit of capitalist America, has not lasted even two years.

On this side of the Atlantic, the bourgeois experts claim to believe that the whole trouble derives from the deficit in the U. S. balance of payments. If the house of the dollar were "put in order," everything would presumably be for the best in this bourgeois best of all possible worlds. The disingenuous advo-

74

cates of this view forget that in 1970, with a record military budget and an inflation rate of 6 percent annually, 25 percent of U. S. productive capacity went unutilized. They forget, in other words, that the cause of the trouble is not inflation but the inherent contradictions of the capitalist system. The absurd survival of private ownership of the means of production and the commodity character of products means that they can only reach the "ultimate consumer" if they are sold, and sold, moreover, at a price that assures their owner the average rate of profit.

Both inflation and the Vietnam war, in the last analysis, are only a consequence of this chronic disease eating away at the vitals of declining capitalism — the widening gap between the society's productive capacity and the buying power of the workers. The formidable inflationary pyramid was erected long before the Vietnam war — which only accelerated its growth — in order to overcome this gap. With the U. S. facing six million unemployed even in spite of this inflation, the friendly advice of the European banks to halt the inflationary trend merits a short, four-letter reply. Where would the European capitalist economy be today with twelve or fifteen million unemployed in the United States?

But those on the U. S. side of the Atlantic who pretend not to understand what the fuss is all about are no less naive. "A mere technical problem caused by speculation," they declare to console themselves. Really? In a society based on private property and thus on competition, the rich (it makes little difference whether they are speculators, bankers, industrialists, or coupon-clippers) are impelled to unload any consistently depreciating currency.

If the dollar is in crisis, it is not only because it is depreciating. It is above all because it is depreciating faster than other currencies (first of all the deutsche mark and the Swiss franc). It is not speculation but the uneven rate of inflation that has led at last to the breakdown of the system of fixed exchange rates established at Bretton Woods.

The most notable aspect of this affair is that the main speculators have been the multinational companies, that is, above all the big American companies with numerous subsidiaries abroad. *Thus, it is the American capitalists themselves who are speculating against the dollar, as it was the British capitalists who speculated against the pound sterling five years ago.* The capitalists have just one fatherland — the realm of fastest possible profits.

But both the American and European capitalists are fooling

themselves, or more precisely fooling their public, because they give only one side of the reality, only one aspect of the situation arising in fact from the insurmountable dilemma noted above.

Today West Germany holds exchange reserves greater *in absolute terms* than those of the United States. The sensational climb of West German imperialism back to a position of dominance in capitalist Europe — already foreshadowed by the role of the Bonn cabinet in the last monetary crisis — is now being openly flaunted. The German bankers have in fact decided unilaterally to devalue the dollar — that is the underlying meaning of last week's crisis. The fact that they can do this on their own, that they can impose their will, is a measure of how much has changed in the capitalist world in the last ten years.

But the capitalists across the Rhine do not find their victory in the least reassuring. They have not succeeded in bringing their "little Europe" associates into the project of monetary consolidation. Even the post-Gaullists are saying — a bit belatedly — that a wobbly "greater Europe," with a British counterbalance to German hegemony, is better than a "little Europe" forever under the thumb of Frankfurt and the Ruhr.

The Common Market is experiencing the gravest crisis of its history. The projected monetary and industrial integration — which was supposed to make it possible to create a European currency taking the place of the pound sterling and, who knows, perhaps even the dollar, as an international reserve currency — seems seriously compromised.

The fact is that in the monetary tempest, in view of the purely incipient stage reached by the interpenetration of European capital, every monetary crisis touches off the classic reaction of "sacrosanct self-interest" so characteristic of the private property system. Let me quote myself once again, this time from something I wrote in 1968: "While inflation — so long as it remains moderate — is not incompatible with a more or less normal functioning of monopoly capitalism in the principal imperialist countries, it contains the danger of increasingly disturbing the world exchanges as soon as it provokes a serious crisis in the international monetary system through the inflation of international reserve currencies. This is the stage now making its debut in the history of neocapitalism. The imperialist powers will search for and apply partial remedies. Each of the remedies will reflect, apart from any desire to reform the system itself, the special competitive interests existing at each specific stage. Inflation itself will not be throttled." [29]

The French capitalists who had already profited from the

devaluation of the franc to improve their positions on the foreign market—above all in Germany—are now hoping to widen their outlets again thanks to the fixed parity of the franc. This calculation is shortsighted. The policy of monetary stabilization decided on by the Bonn cabinet, under the pressure of the banks, threatens to show up as a recession in Germany. And a German recession would mean not an expansion but a contraction of French exports.

The whole precarious stabilizing maneuver now in progress— much more precarious now than even in the fall of 1968 and in 1969—has one single fundamental aim: to make the workers, above all, the American and German workers, pay the costs of "the fight against inflation." While inflation is the cause and not the consequence of wage demands, the latter are the favorite targets of the "stabilizers." On this point at least, the Nixon administration, the Pompidou regime, Mr. Heath, and Professor Schiller [the West German economics minister] are unanimously agreed: "The unions must moderate their demands."

Because the monetary crisis combines with a serious slowdown in economic growth (three of the major imperialist countries are now in a recession—the USA, Great Britain, and Italy—and a fourth, Japan, has just barely avoided one), the margin of maneuver for the "social conciliators" is shrinking singularly. The result of this narrowing economic leeway has been an open attack on the right to strike in Great Britain and thinly veiled threats of a similar assault in the United States. In Germany, the Social Democrats are going to change their "stance" fundamentally in the coming weeks in an effort to knock "some sense" into the heads of union leaders caught between two fires—the pressures for "moderation" from Bonn and the radicalizing pressures from the rank and file (i. e., the wildcat and warning strikes of the fall of 1969 and 1970).

It is well to remember that everything that happens in the capitalist economy is not the simple result of automatic mechanisms. The economic class struggle is an important factor, as is the revolutionary struggle. The present crisis results not only from dwindling reserves and sharpening internal contradictions in the system. It also reflects the heroic struggle of the Vietnamese popular masses, which has cost imperialism tens of billions of dollars. Likewise, it reflects the revolutionary flareup of May 1968 in France, the "hot autumn" in Italy, the wildcat strikes in Germany and many European countries, and the rise in the combativity of the workers in Great Britain throughout 1970. The monetary crisis is the reflection of an economic and social system whose very foundations are increasingly under attack.

The long period of neocapitalist expansion and "prosperity" is a thing of the past. The thin cows are following the fat ones. And if the fat cows did not prevent May 1968, the years of the thin cows are preparing still other surprises. "Let the workers pay"? But the Western working class is not ready to pay. It is not demoralized. Its combativity is not on the wane. It has suffered no great defeats. The decline of the dollar foreshadows a rise in workers' struggles, including the American workers. The worsening international monetary crisis is a serious invitation to meet the international speculations of the capitalists with an international workers' struggle.

May 10, 1971

The Deepening Crisis
of the Imperialist System

From the September 6, 1971, issue of Intercontinental Press. *Originally appeared in the July 1971 issue of the French bimonthly* Quatrieme Internationale *as sections I and II of its editorial. Translated by* Intercontinental Press.

I.

The main symptom today of the worsening of the general crisis of the world imperialist system is the serious deterioration in the position of the international capitalist economy. Of the seven principal imperialist powers, three — the United States, Italy, and Great Britain — are at grips with a recession. That is, there has been a decline in industrial production in these countries by comparison with the same period last year. In Canada, the recession may be over after the second quarter of 1971. A fifth power, West Germany, is on an uncertain course. Since the fall of 1970, signs pointing to a recession have multiplied. But, in part, these symptoms have been neutralized by a new spurt in production, especially of consumer goods for the domestic market. For the moment it is hard to predict whether this spurt represents a temporary interruption in a declining movement, or whether, to the contrary, it will develop into a new general upturn. And the economic situation in France and the Benelux countries hinges in the immediate future on what happens in Germany.

In the case of Japan, although its economy is still in a phase of expansion, its rate of growth has been in a marked decline since the fall of 1970. Excess capacity and accumulating inventories have appeared above all in the electronics industry (1.5 million unsold color TV sets!), electrical appliances, and petrochemicals. In 1970, the number of business failures rose to the record figure of 9,500.

The deterioration in the capitalist international economic situation can be gauged by two phenomena that have appeared on a scale unprecedented in the entire period since the "Korean-war boom": the spread of unemployment, and the prolonged refusal of the big monopolistic concerns to resume investing in response to monetary "incentives."

The total number of unemployed workers in the seven main imperialist powers must approach 10 million today, a figure never attained since the second world war (5 million in the U. S., 1.5 million in Italy, 1 million in Japan, 800,000 in Great Britain, 700,000 in Canada, 500,000 in France; there is no unemployment in West Germany). [30] The rate of unemployment is much higher than the average in some regions (the northwest of the United States, southern Italy, Scotland, Quebec and British Columbia in Canada, etc.), where it easily reaches 8 percent or more of the total work force. It is much higher most of all among the youth. The United States is now experiencing an unemployed rate of 17.2 percent in the youth as a whole and 35 percent among Black youth.

To combat recession, the capitalist governments are continuing to resort to Keynesian and neo-Keynesian techniques. All these techniques come down in the last analysis to a single factor — creating inflationary buying power. This method makes it possible to prevent a recession from snowballing through a chain reaction of effects. The downturn is halted at a certain plateau (by paying the price of a new inflationary thrust, and of a new deterioration of the international monetary system when the dollar — the reserve currency of this system — is swept into the whirlwind). But creating inflationary buying power does not bring an automatic revival of industrial production. This is the second weakness of the Keynesian practices, besides their inflationary character.

In the United States, the monetary volume rose by 6 percent in 1970. Industrial production declined or hovered at its old level. During the first quarter of 1971, the volume of money even increased at a rate that would average 11 percent annually. Industrial production stagnated and then fell. The reasons for this lag in production responding to monetary "stimuli" are, however, not mysterious. The volume of industrial production depends essentially on productive investment. Under the capitalist system, productive investment by the big monopolies is determined *both* by market trends and fluctuations in the rate of profit. In order to induce the big concerns to increase their investments, *both* an expanding market and prospects for a rise in the rate of profit are needed. When the rate of profit is falling, when industry shows excess productive capacity in many areas, even a major expansion of the market offers no incentive for an upturn in productive investments, insofar as no trend appears toward a change in the factors cited above.

It must be added that this deterioration in the international economic situation of capitalism is occurring at a time when military expenditures have reached an unprecedented total and when even Japan—which up till now had stayed largely outside the arms race—has thrown itself into accelerated rearmament. It is therefore unlikely that a new increase in these expenditures can extricate the capitalist economy from its immediate difficulties. In order to achieve this, military spending would have to be raised to a level that even the United States could not sustain in "peacetime."

The capitalists will thus follow a different tack. Their response will be concentrated in two areas. They will try to increase their foreign markets and to boost the rate of profit at the expense of the working class. Increasing international markets means expanding East-West trade, with the U. S. joining in the game (relaxing embargoes against the USSR, resuming exports to China). Likewise, it means stepped-up penetration of the markets of semicolonial countries and a new sharpening of interimperialist competition. The attempt to raise the rate of profit at the expense of the working class involves trying to limit or abolish the only substantial right the workers have under the capitalist system, the right of collective bargaining. The means for this are "incomes policies," which virtually all tendencies in the international bourgeoisie have begun to demand. From the standpoint of the capitalists, increased unemployment serves the specific function of inducing the workers to accept such a policy more or less passively. Accelerated cooption of the trade union leaderships into the bourgeois state is to aid bringing about the same result. If the unions prove too recalcitrant—that is, if growing militancy on the part of their memberships forces the union bureaucracies to put up a fight—then antiunion and antistrike laws must deal with this lack of understanding.

It follows from this that the deterioration in the economic situation of capitalism must be reflected in an aggravation of class contradictions in the imperialist as well as in the colonial and semicolonial countries. This sharpening, which has been in progress since May 1968, will rise to a new level. The general crisis of the imperialist system must not, moreover, be understood as an economic crisis of overproduction (this is only one of its periodic aspects). It must be seen rather as a general breakdown of stability in which revolutionary explosions, liberation movements of oppressed peoples, the class struggle of the proletariat, the tensions between the imperialist powers, monetary crises, so-called cultural crises, and conflicts with the bureaucratized workers' states all merge in a unified process that is increasingly undermining the cohesiveness of the system.

II.

The main peculiarity exhibited by the current deepening of the general crisis of the imperialist system is that all the forces present are tending to focus on precipitating a major social crisis in the United States itself.

American imperialism came out of the second world war as the absolute master of the capitalist world, enjoying marked economic and military superiority over the "socialist camp." The enormous superprofits it accumulated during and after the war, and its great reserves, enabled it to hold the undisputed leadership of the bourgeois world for twenty years, albeit with growing difficulties. It vigorously pursued its domestic accumulation of capital, modernizing its industry. It "revived" capitalism in West Europe and Japan, aided by the Stalinist and reformist bureaucracies who betrayed the postwar revolutionary upsurge. It set out to conquer the old colonial empires that were breaking up and the internal markets of its principal allies and competitors, exporting six billion dollars in capital for this purpose. It served as the world policeman of the capitalist system, surrounding the USSR and the "people's democracies" with a network of military bases, maintaining a historically unprecedented military establishment at home and abroad, dotting the world with counterrevolutionary "relay stations" that it financed and equipped. It prevented a sharpening of social contradictions in the U. S. assuring an important part of the American working class a rising standard of living. It bought off the trade union bureaucracy, while limiting the latter's power by the Taft-Hartley Act and integrating the unions into its policy of world-wide expansion (the cold war, McCarthyism, etc.).

For several years now the limits to the power of American imperialism have been revealing themselves very clearly. It has begun to suffer repeated defeats. It has proved incapable of checking the rise of the permanent revolution in Latin America, after failing to crush the victorious Cuban revolution. It has been unable to defeat the heroic resistance of the Vietnamese masses, who are determined to continue their revolution and carry it through to victory. American imperialism has been unable to prevent a deterioration in the relationship of forces with its principal competitors, especially those in the Common Market dominated by West German imperialism. It has been unable to prevent the awakening of Black youth, which has resulted on the one hand in the ghetto rebellions and on the other in a growing radicalization of the entire student youth. It has been unable to prevent the rise of a powerful antiwar movement, the most powerful yet seen in the history of colonial wars. The permanent deficit in the U. S. balance of payments and the resulting chronic crisis of the international monetary system and of the dollar are concentrated expressions of all these failures. *These developments reflect the growing incapacity of American imperialism to meet simultaneously all the tasks imposed on it in the post-1945 period by its predominance over the capitalist world.* They mark the beginning of the decline of this supremacy.

The expenditure of enormous amounts of capital to finance the war in Vietnam, to maintain a constantly expanding military establishment, to finance the counterrevolutionary relay stations around the world, and to buy up the property of capitalist enterprises in foreign countries have all resulted finally in holding back steady modernization in some important industries. In these branches (steel, naval construction, electrical appliances, and even automobile production in part), the U. S.'s main competitors now have the most advanced technology. In particular, capital has been lacking for reducing the social contradictions in the U. S., for raising real wages, for building schools, cheap housing, and hospitals.

The results of this are visible to the naked eye. Under the combined pressure of inflation and rising taxes, the real wages of the American workers have not increased in four years. The big cities are literally rotting. Entire layers of the American population — youth, Blacks, Chicanos, women — have gone into open rebellion against the structure of a society that condemns them to second-class citizenship. It is now only a question of time until the mass of the industrial workers join in this rebellion and transform it into an anticapitalist revolutionary force of potentially irresistible power.

The most perceptive layers of the American bourgeoisie are perfectly aware of this prospect and the dangers it holds for the survival of their system. The crisis of leadership now agitating this bourgeoisie reflects the need they feel for a reorientation. It also reflects the internal contradictions (determined in part by conflicting material interests and in part by differing judgments and political choices) that must be resolved

before such a reorientation can be achieved. From now until
the presidential elections at the end of 1972, the political life
of the U. S. will be dominated by the bourgeoisie's exertions
to dam up the terrifying social crisis that is ripening in the
United States. In this it will endeavor to "reintegrate" into the
system at least a part of the rebel forces that have revealed
themselves, to reduce American imperialism's share of the
costs of defending the world capitalist system, and to reinforce its competitive position, which has deteriorated vis-
a-vis its allies and commercial rivals. Essentially, this means
that American imperialism is going to export to the other
capitalist powers a part of the financial, economic, and social
costs imposed by the overall crisis of the imperialist system,
and that it is going to try to use part of the resources freed
in this way to reduce the internal social contradictions in the
United States.

Washington's threat to withdraw its troops gradually from
Europe and Japan will probably be sufficient to force the West
European and Japanese imperialists to assume the military
defense of "free enterprise" in Europe and Asia. In return, the
European imperialists (the Japanese will find this more difficult) will get their autonomous nuclear "striking force." French
and British nuclear arms will form the axis of this weapons
system, and its development will be facilitated by the entry
of Great Britain into the Common Market.

Likewise, in order to strengthen the dollar, American imperialism will combine increased protectionism with a slowdown in real capital outflows and a new effort to retool American industry aimed at regaining a margin of technological
and productive superiority over its main European and Japanese competitors. The European bourgeoisie will respond
by redoubling its efforts to form its own "multinational corporations." Only such international combines have any chance
of successfully opposing the multinational corporations dominated by U. S. capital (which explains why the French bourgeoisie finally abandoned the Gaullist veto against Great Britain's entry into the Common Market).

Sensing this danger, the Soviet bureaucracy has gone into
high gear in its fight to get a "conference on European security" and to encourage all the capitalist forces in Europe that
are hesitating in the face of this formidable endeavor (an endeavor that cannot fail to provoke sharper class struggles).
In this, the Kremlin has gotten a more favorable response
than in the past, not only in the European Social Democratic
parties but even in NATO. American imperialism is not opposed a priori to seeing the military and political strength

of the European imperialist powers temporarily weakened so that it can reinforce its position for blackmailing and pressuring these countries. But the logic of the class struggle will ultimately prove stronger than all these diplomatic maneuvers.

While the crisis American imperialism is now experiencing reflects the fact that its reserves are becoming depleted by comparison with the demands of the enormous tasks it is required to carry out simultaneously, it must not be deduced from this that these reserves have completely disappeared. Although American predominance is on the wane, U. S. imperialism still retains an important margin of superiority over all its main competitors. No force outside the country can prevent the American bourgeoisie from regaining a new temporary equilibrium, at the cost, essentially, of its main competitors. The most formidable obstacle in the way of achieving this equilibrium lies in the United States itself.

The present radicalization is much deeper than the one in the 1930s. It embraces the most exploited and oppressed sectors of bourgeois society — above all the Blacks and Chicanos — whose demands cannot be met without turning this society upside down. The reserves of American imperialism are smaller than they were forty years ago; American society is more profoundly integrated into the worldwide economy and class struggle. This means that the bourgeoisie has less leeway for making concessions to the workers than it had during the last radicalization. The Roosevelt coalition was built on granting concessions to the unions, to the aristocracy of the working class and the trade union bureaucracy. By means of these concessions, and above all thanks to the treacherous role played by the Stalinists, the mass movement was reintegrated into the two-party system.

Today such concessions are harder to give. The influence of reformist tendencies like the Communist Party is much more restricted than in the time of Roosevelt. Thus, it will be all the more difficult to reintegrate this powerful movement of rebellion into the two-party system. In the last analysis, the American bourgeoisie's ability to halt the ripening social crisis before it reaches the point of shaking the foundations of the capitalist structure will depend on the outcome of the struggle for leadership of these rebel forces. In this, the contest between those elements striving to reintegrate these forces into the bourgeois political system and those centering their activity on mobilizing the workers, the exploited, and the oppressed in independent, anticapitalist mass action will be decisive. Only a victory by the former can enable the American bourgeoisie to repeat its achievement of the 1930s.

The Downfall of the Dollar

From the September 6, 1971, issue of Intercontinental Press. *Written in response to Nixon's announcement of his "New Economic Policy" August 15, 1971.*

The July issue of *Quatreme Internationale* carried an editorial dated July 5, 1971, on the worsening crisis of imperialism. [31] The following sentences are of particular interest:

"The capitalists will thus follow a different tack. Their response [to a recession that threatens to become general] will be concentrated in two areas. They will try to increase their foreign markets and to boost the rate of profit at the expense of the working class.

"Increasing international markets means expanding East-West trade, with the U. S. joining in the game (relaxing embargoes against the USSR, resuming exports to China). Likewise, it means stepped-up penetration of the markets of semicolonial countries and a new sharpening of interimperialist competition. The attempt to raise the rate of profit at the expense of the working class involves trying to limit or abolish the only substantial right the workers have under the capitalist system, the right of collective bargaining. The means for this are 'incomes policies,' which virtually all tendencies in the international bourgeoisie have begun to demand."

And further on:

". . . in order to strengthen the dollar, American imperialism will combine increased protectionism with a slowdown in real capital outflows and a new effort to retool American industry. . . ."

Six weeks later, these forecasts were borne out by the decisions Nixon announced to the world August 15, 1971.

The Marxist analysis of the class nature of the American state, of the fundamental nature of the capitalist system, has been confirmed once again. The American bourgeoisie defends its class interests — not an ideal of freedom. This defense is mounted today not only against the states that have broken

86

out of the imperialist system and against the colonial revolution that threatens to take several more countries along the same road. It is directed against what is historically the most redoubtable enemy of Wall Street — the American proletariat. It is aimed at shaking up Wall Street's most precious "allies," that is, its most efficient competitors — Japan, Western Germany. "Freedom," including the famous free trade, is swept aside, as is always the case when the system founded on private property, that is, competition and anarchy, is shaken by a serious crisis.

For three and a half years we have been witnessing the slow death agony of the international monetary system founded at Bretton Woods under the banner of supremacy of the dollar. This system sought to escape from the dilemma that has confronted the capitalist economy since the beginning of its historic crisis of decline marked by the first world war: either maintenance of the gold standard with more and more catastrophic crises of overproduction; or abandonment of the gold standard and a retreat toward economic nationalism, protectionism, and inconvertible currencies, which signifies not less disastrous consequences for capitalist international trade. The solution consisted of basing capitalist currencies both on gold and on the dollar, of maintaining stable rates of exchange, and of installing flexible rules, tolerating in reality a permanent inflation, above all whenever a crisis of overproduction impended, in order to avoid a new 1929.

So long as the inflation remained moderate, and the dollar lost its purchasing power at a slower rate than the currencies of the other important imperialist powers, the system functioned to the satisfaction of all the imperialists. Already at that time, it is true, the arrangement signified a more and more ruinous indebtedness for the semicolonial countries, the big losers at Bretton Woods. But that the "great" should exploit the "small" is the most natural of all things in the capitalist world.

No imperialist complained about the deficit in the U. S. balance of payments in the fifties — and with reason! Without this deficit, the system invented at Bretton Woods would not have been able to function. The capitalist expansion would have died for lack of dollars and gold, that is, of means of international payment.

Things began to turn sour not because of inflation of the dollar — that had been going on uninterruptedly for thirty years. Things began to turn sour when the decline in buying power of the dollar became greater than that of other currencies, when the rest of the world's holdings in dollars expanded out of all

proportion to the rapidly diminishing stock of gold held by
the U. S. From then on, it was clear that devaluation of the
dollar would occur sooner or later. The international bourgeoisie—including a good part of big business in the U. S.,
whether through the multinational companies directly or
through go-betweens—began to ready themselves for this contingency. In plain language, this is called speculating on devaluation of the dollar. And in a market economy, when many
capitalists ready themselves for a contingency, they precipitate
it with a sure hand.

The inconvertibility of the dollar into gold—a consequence
of the disproportion between dollar holdings in the hands
of foreigners and the gold reserve at Fort Knox, which shrank
to the "minimum strategic reserve" of $10 billion—did not
begin on August 15, 1971. It has been the reality since the
end of the "gold pool" (March 1968). From that time on, the
central banks of the big imperialist powers have in reality
stopped exchanging dollars for gold. What was a provisional
mutual undertaking has now become a definitive rule because
of Nixon's decision.

The real change announced August 15 was thus not the inconvertibility of the dollar, already in force for three years.
The real change was the factual devaluation of the dollar, not
in relation to gold but in relation to the other currencies of
the imperialist world. Nixon's decision to let the dollar "float"
signifies in reality a decision to depreciate the dollar in relation
to other currencies. Because once supply and demand is per-
mitted to operate freely on the exchange market, this outcome
is inevitable in view of the current state of inflation of the
U. S. dollar in relation to the currencies of the principal competitors of the United States.

The irony of history is that in thundering against the "international speculators," Nixon gave in to them all along the line.
It was exactly this depreciation that they were prepared for.
In affirming that he was out to defend the stability of the dollar, Nixon did exactly the contrary. He acknowledged *urbi
et orbi* [32] that the dollar has been devaluated. Double-talk
comes naturally to the American bourgeois politicians just
as it does to the gangsters of the star-spangled republic.

In European capitalist circles—beginning with the Gaullists
in France—the devaluation of the dollar is being denounced
as a serious blow against trade for Europe and for Japan.
It is certain that Nixon's immediate aim is protectionist in
nature. It is designed to help American exports and make
imports to the United States more difficult. But these same

circles forget that in the capitalist system, money is not only a means of exchange but a means of payment. Dollars serve not only for world trade; they also serve for the export of capital. What American capitalism gains in the "commodities" column, it loses in the "capital" column. From now on, American capitalism will need more dollars to buy a factory in Europe. And a German or Japanese capitalist will be able to buy a factory in the United States with fewer deutsche marks and yen.

That is why American imperialism long resisted the temptation to devaluate. The Gaullists, who have spouted for a long time against the Yankees for buying "our" factories, are decidedly inconsistent in their ideas. Yesterday's complaints are forgotten in exchange for the new complaints. Today, what is involved above all is to protect "our" foreign markets and to sell "our" goods. If not, unemployment will rise in France and along with it the threat of a new May 1968 at the door.

The different reactions of the various imperialist powers is tied in with their particular interests and their respective levels of power. The West German capitalists, who are the strongest, do not fear a new minor revaluation of the deutsche mark (an inevitable consequence of floating exchange). The British, who are the weakest, are seeking to profit from the confusion and carry out a discreet new devaluation of the pound. The Italians, the most threatened socially, wish above all to avoid any change in the lira.

As for the French capitalists, who benefited from the effects of the devaluation of the franc during the West German boom, they would like to keep their cake while eating it. Their "two-tier exchange" [33] means that French exports would profit from a lower exchange rate for the franc, while the movement of French capital would profit from the lower exchange rate of the dollar.

Such a system, possible in a small country for a short time, quickly becomes impractical in a more important imperialist power. It opens the way to all kinds of speculation, gambling on the stock market, illicit trading, and outright frauds. Just who is to compel an exporter to repatriate his deutsche marks in a "commodities" column when he can obtain a larger sum of francs in a "capital" column? Just who is to check up on fictitious imports designed to obtain deutsche marks at a good price to be resold at a higher rate on the "free market"?

The fact that after twenty years of expanding international capitalist trade—which, it should be noted, had only by 1965 brought per capita exports back up to the level of 1913—complete anarchy, insecurity, and disorder again reign says a lot about the insoluble historic crisis shaking the system that survives in the West, thanks to the traditional labor leaders!

Marx liked to repeat that monetary phenomena were only reflections of the economic life, and whoever sought to explain crises essentially by these phenomena, was mistaking the appearance for the reality. This observation remains as valid as ever. When the dollar is depreciated, when the international monetary system set up at Bretton Woods goes down, this is above all not because of wicked speculators, of too imprudent creditors, or too prudent bankers (especially in other countries!). It is not because money is "badly managed" or because the advice of Professor Rueff has not been followed, or because one has not gone back to the exalted philosophy of the French peasants and kept one's savings in a sock, or hidden in a washing machine, in the form of gold coins. It is because the economic system as a whole is sick.

The fundamental cause of the inflation is the indebtedness of governments, businesses, and consumers. This indebtedness has been mushrooming since 1940 (that of the governments since 1914). Without this indebtedness and this permanent inflation, expansion, full employment, economic growth have become impossible in a capitalist system in decline. The armaments economy is the basis of state indebtedness. Abnormally swollen credit is the basis of private indebtedness. For thirty years, neocapitalist "prosperity" has ridden on an ocean of credit. Sooner or later waves of inflation were bound to engulf the ship. The collapse of the dollar has shown that the "stabilizers," constructed with such pain, were no longer able to resist the smashing of these ever more powerful waves.

Capitalist prosperity depends on two conditions — a rising rate of profit and an expanding market. The logic of capitalism is such that these conditions coincide only at certain moments. When they coincide temporarily, this in itself creates the conditions for their subsequent separation. The two coincide momentarily during the course of each economic cycle and periodically on a more general and durable scale. Since 1966, we have entered a long period in which the coinciding of the two is being undermined more and more.

To emerge from the recession that has been hitting the American economy for the past two years, Nixon requested Congress to give a tax credit on investments and to repeal an excise tax on automobiles. The industrialists and bankers, as well as not a few "liberal" politicians, applauded. What's good for profits is good for the United States. Who would dare think otherwise in the paradise of "free enterprise"?

Right-wing trade union figures like George Meany protested under pressure from the ranks. What about the freeze on dividends and undistributed profits as a counterweight to the freeze on wages? Where are the guarantees against rises in prices? Where is the compensation for *past* losses in buying power already sustained by the wage workers?

These protests signify that the American workers are going to battle harder for their standard of living, threatened by inflation, taxes, the consequences of the war in Vietnam, and the repercussions that can be counted on as the American bosses seek to answer international competition. They signify longer and harder strikes. But not only that. They involve above all a new contraction of the domestic American market (the reductions in public expenditures and the increased cost of imported products both serve to reduce overall buying power already under full retraction).

How is unemployment to be wiped out under these conditions? Moreover, don't the bosses at bottom want to maintain unemployment in order to hold down wages? But under these conditions, how can the economy be genuinely started up again (and, in passing, assure Nixon's reelection next year)?

The European capitalists are not without guile. They point their fingers at American protectionism, They have become the attorneys of free trade. But at the least economic shock, they too will come out foursquare for sacred self-interest. They will defend their foreign outlets by devaluations one after the other (French franc, pound sterling) or by stabilization measures (deutsche mark) which will end up by provoking unemployment either at home or among neighboring countries. With Wall Street playing some of its trump cards, the reaction in the Common Market was *every man for himself* to such a degree that the European bourgeoisie could not lay out any collective defense against American protectionism. Big business may well end up by compelling its politicians to act in the sense of closer European "solidarity" out of fear that Uncle Sam will export his unemployment to the old continent. But how to divide the risks, the losses, and the profits of such solidarity? This is the subject of the current bargaining.

Under these conditions, it is excluded that the inflation will stop. A recession that threatens to become general, increasing unemployment, excess capacity hitting a half dozen key industries, cannot be combined with a halt to inflation except at the price of a new 1929, a price that no imperialist power is ready to pay. But persistent inflation joined to exacerbated international competition signifies an erosion of the international monetary system that can no longer be averted. This means that an interimperialist agreement on a sufficient new international reserve money is impossible. And that makes certain the threat that the growth of international trade will be slowed down. The conclusion is accentuation of the reversal of the 1945-65 expansionist tendency.

The violent perturbation of the dollar means more than devaluation of a symbol and a monetary system. The international capitalist system as a whole has emerged from a long cycle of expansion to begin a long cycle of much slower growth and many more crises. In reality, since the German recession of 1966-67, the international capitalist economy has not had a single year of general prosperity. There has not been a single year without a recession or monetary crisis somewhere. The merry-go-round has only begun. The long cycles last on the average twenty to twenty-five years.

If the workers so desire, if they provide themselves with a revolutionary leadership that is up to the height of the historic task, this cycle can give rise to the victory of socialism in the West. If their struggles end in defeats because of lack of an adequate leadership, then capitalism will seek to resolve its structural crisis on their flesh and bones, as it did during the thirties and forties. The crisis that has begun is thus both a promise and a warning.

August 24, 1971

The Monetary Crisis Continues

From the January 10, 1972, issue of Intercontinental Press. *An agreement between the ten most powerful capitalist powers on a general realignment of currency exchange rates had been reached on December 18, 1971, in Washington, D. C.*

For the family photo, the finance ministers of the world's ten richest imperialist countries put on beaming smiles. After four months of confusion and uncertainty about the future of the international monetary system, the world capitalist economy had finally achieved new schedules of fixed rates of exchange between all the imperialist currencies. The ministries and administrative councils must have been seized with a strong feeling of panic for the principal interests to appear so satisfied with the miserable compromise that was reached in Washington. If the rates of exchange were reorganized, none of the basic roots of the monetary crisis were eliminated.

On August 15, 1971, Nixon issued an edict. But on December 18 a compromise was reached, after arduous negotiations. "Neither victor nor vanquished," proclaimed this same Nixon. This compromise reflects the change in the interimperialist relation of forces that has evolved over the past decade.

American big capital achieved a general revaluation of all imperialist currencies in relation to the dollar. If some of these were significant (16.9 percent for the yen, 13.6 percent for the deutsche mark), they were in general less than those the Nixon administration had expected. They favor the export of American commodities, but will reduce the export of American capital. Above all, they will facilitate the export of European and Japanese capital to the United States.

Nixon's promises and blustering to the contrary, the dollar was in fact devalued — in relation to gold and all currencies that will not themselves devalue. The devaluation will reduce the already shaken confidence of world bankers in the stability of the dollar. (Several East European countries will sustain a loss because they imprudently converted their re-

93

serves into dollars, as the Chinese government sustained a
loss when it, also imprudently, placed its reserves in French
francs before the franc's devaluation.) And — depending on
the number of semicolonial countries that likewise devalue
their currencies — the devaluation of the dollar will raise prices,
more or less, on imports of raw materials and the products
of light industry coming from those countries.

The international monetary system remains in crisis. The
two principal roots of this crisis have not at all been eliminated.
The dollar is still not exchangeable for gold. If the capitalist
central banks continue to turn their backs on the dollar as a
reserve currency — and how could they do otherwise in the
wake of such a devaluation! — the international capitalist economy will find itself deprived of an international exchange currency. In addition, the American inflation continues worse than
ever, as the Nixon administration tries at all costs to prevent
the recession from being transformed into a grave economic
crisis. The American balance of payments deficit will thus
also persist, even if it becomes partially attenuated.

In regard to the 10 percent surcharge on imports imposed
by Nixon on August 15, it must be said that this had little
weight in reducing imports, attracted by the abundance of
liquidity. As a result, prices rose generally as a consequence
of the increase in imports. Certain of these, especially in the
area of machinery, could not be substituted, moreover, since
the American machine industry does not produce (or no longer
produces) some equipment made mostly in Germany and Japan.

From the capitalist point of view the most reasonable way
out of the impasse would be to bolster gold by an international reserve currency completely detached from the national
economy of any capitalist country — a central bank currency
administered, according to strictly objective criteria, by a central bank of the central banks. But that would be a complete
utopia. The realization of such a program presupposes the
existence of a world capitalist government independent of the
great imperialist powers; that is, the disappearance of interimperialist competition. But it is precisely the exacerbation
of that competition that has been manifested since the opening of the monetary crisis.

In the absence of an overall solution, the most the imperialist
powers can hope for is a gradual extension of the system of
Special Drawing Rights ("paper gold," distributed according
to the notion that the richest countries should get the lion's
share). Moreover, the imperialist countries of the Common

Market (reinforced by Great Britain, which has consistently aligned itself with the Six during the monetary crisis) will seek to create a common currency which, all things being equal, could be added to the dollar as an international reserve currency, aimed at supplanting the dollar. But this is not for tomorrow or the day after.

The European and Japanese capitalists did not dare cut the limb they were sitting on—to reply to Nixon's edict with massive retaliatory measures would have run the risk of touching off a chain reaction which, by contracting the world market and aggravating the American recession, could have ended by seriously striking at their own outlets. Today, in face of the Washington compromise, they have decided to grin and bear it, with the exception of the German industrialists. For them, this is their third revaluation in a short time. They fear a massive invasion of American products and a relative decline in German exports.

France-Soir ran a triumphant headline: "Crisis and unemployment averted." The demagogy is surprising, even coming from a daily of this type. Far from being averted, unemployment in France has reached its highest level in twenty years, and this is even before a recession. And recession (that is, a crisis) threatens France not because of the monetary crisis but because of the mounting West German recession. There is not the slightest sign that the German recession disappeared after December 18. Everything indicates that it will extend through next winter and spring.

The deterioration of the international capitalist economic situation is not a result of the monetary crisis, but preceded it and in part accelerated its outbreak. The causes of the present recession are more profound—the slackening of technological innovation; the excess capacity in key sectors like steel, auto, petrochemicals, synthetic textiles, naval construction, and undoubtedly also electronics; the fall of the average rate of profit and the consequent decline in investment; the growing gap between the capacity of production and buying power, compounded by increasingly massive indebtedness of both families and companies. In short, all the classic contradictions of capitalism have reappeared. Monetary and financial manipulations may at the very most moderate their immediate effects, but can neither eliminate nor render them harmless in the long run.

Under these conditions the two predictions we made immediately after the August 15, 1971, decree stand entirely confirmed: First, that the international bourgeoisie would try to make the workers foot the bill for the damages. The offensive against levels of employment and real wages has now become general. The vigorous response of the West German metal-workers demonstrates that this offensive is not at all assured of success. Second, that international competition would accelerate and undermine all agreements, including monetary ones. The Bretton Woods system lasted twenty-five years, the last five in death agony. The system born in Washington will not survive a decade. The next recession or the next social explosion in an important imperialist country threatens to precipitate its decomposition.

December 20, 1971

Part 2

The Crisis of the International Monetary System

From the March-April 1969 issue of the International Socialist Review. *The articles in Part I of this book analyze each major stage of the developing international monetary crisis from 1964 to 1971. This article provides a more general treatment of the subject.*

The crisis in the international monetary system — foreseen by Marxists at a time when the apologists for neocapitalism were convinced that the capitalist mode of production had solved its basic contradictions — is now taking the form of convulsions that follow each other with increasing rapidity: the crisis of the pound sterling, followed by its devaluation in November 1967; the crisis of the dollar in March 1968, followed by establishment of the "two tier" price system for gold; the crisis of the French franc, accompanied by its masked devaluation, a masked revaluation of the German mark; and a new sterling crisis in November 1968. It is necessary to examine the nature and functioning of the international monetary system founded on the gold exchange standard and to relate its crisis to the fundamental contradictions rending the world capitalist system in our epoch.

Gold, the gold standard and paper money
Precious metals in general and gold in particular can serve as means of exchange and means of payment because they have value, since they are products of human labor. The equation "a ton of copper is worth a kilo of gold" means that it takes the same number of hours of labor of average productivity to produce these two quantities of metal. In a monetary system based on the gold standard, the prices of goods express equivalences of the same kind. In such a system, if $1 equals 0.5 grams of gold, the statement that an average car is worth $5,000 means that as many hours of labor are required to produce a car as to produce 2.5 kg. of gold.
A feature of the capitalist system is the unceasing upheaval in labor techniques, the manifold revolutions in the productivity

of labor. These upheavals come about through the *uneven* development of different industrial enterprises and different industrial sectors. Through capitalist competition and the equalization of the profit rate, those enterprises and industrial branches in which labor productivity rises above the social average, appropriate a part of the surplus value produced in other enterprises or industrial branches in which work is done below the social average of productivity.

The concrete machanism for transferring surplus value from one enterprise or industrial branch to another is the formation of market prices. The technically advanced enterprises and branches realize superprofits when selling at market prices because their production costs are lower than those of their competitors, but it is their competitors who determine these prices. The technically backward enterprises and branches do not realize the average profit, or they even sell at a loss, because their production costs are greater than those of their competitors, who operate at social average productivity and determine market prices.

However this rule does not operate in the same way with the production of gold. The use of gold as the general equivalent, the fact that the use value of this commodity makes it sought after by *all* owners of commodities, results in a demand for this commodity which is — up to a certain point — *independent* of fluctuations in its own cost of production.

Ordinarily when an industrial branch becomes technically backward relative to the social average, when it "wastes social labor" in the course of current production, a part of its production will find no buyers, despite a considerable drop in price. A part of its productive capacity may even be shut down (a conspicuous case is the coal mining industry in the past decade). But when the capitalist economy is generally expanding, the need for gold increases *as a function of this expansion,* independently of fluctuations in the productivity of labor in the gold mines compared with other industry.[1] The implication of this for owners of gold mines is that they will secure a substantial return (big superprofit) during periods of general expansion in capitalist production, if labor productivity in the mines lags behind productivity in the rest of industry, which has obviously been the case since the beginning of the century.

For a monetary system based on a gold standard, this means that the "secular" decline in the value of commodities is strongly accentuated. Let us assume the equation, 1 car equals 2.5 kg. of gold, equals $5,000, equals 500 hours of labor. If the productivity of labor doubles in the automobile industry *while remaining constant in the gold industry,* this formula becomes 1 car equals 250 hours of labor, equals 1.25 kg. of gold equals $2,500.

We reach a conclusion which at first sight seems paradoxical: a gold standard system condemns prices to drop very sharply as long as the gap continues to increase between relatively stagnant labor productivity in the gold mines and rapid expansion of labor productivity in the rest of industry. What would really paralyze capitalist expansion is not the "low price of gold," as Rueff and Co. believe, or the "lack of international liquidity," but the abnormally high value of gold, and the ever lower price in gold for most commodities.[2]

The paradox is purely superficial. The moment one leaves the regime of a gold standard and enters that of paper money, it is necessary to relate the monetary total to the gold total before one can understand the evolution of commodity prices relative to the precious metal. Now the quantity theory of money, which Marx rejected in connection with metallic money, is partially applicable to paper money. Paper money consists of *monetary tokens.* If a national currency is covered by 1,000 tons of gold and its monetary circulation increases from 35 billion to 50 billion (dollars, francs, etc.), this means that each monetary unit no longer represents 0.03 grams of gold but only 0.02 grams, that is, it has lost a third of its value.

The expression "price of gold," which is obviously meaningless under a pure gold standard, takes on a indirect meaning in a paper money system, where it registers fluctuations in the monetary total and variations in the values of various national currencies in terms of fluctuations of this total.[3] If we disregard the tremendous inflation which has taken place on a universal scale during the past half century, we see that the prices of most commodities in terms of gold prices have really declined considerably.

Does this mean that, under a system of paper money tied to the gold standard, every expansion of the monetary total automatically causes an increase in prices? That would be true only if total production and the productivity of labor remained stable. As soon as production and productivity increase, the monetary total can expand considerably without an increase in prices.

Suppose a national production represented by 1 billion commodity units, whose production has cost 1 billion hours of labor, and which is exchanged for $35 billion, is equivalent to 1,000 tons of gold. If production increases in ten years to 1.5 billion commodity units, produced in 1.5 billion hours of labor, the monetary total may go from $35 billion to $52.5 billion, with a stable gold reserve, and the unit commodity price will remain unchanged.

It is true that each dollar will no longer represent 0.03 grams of gold but only slightly less than 0.02 grams. However, if at the same time labor productivity in all industries except gold has increased by 50 percent, this depreciation of the dollar by 33 percent relative to gold will not represent a decline in purchasing power. It merely expresses the fact that the totality of commodities which are exchanged against the same quantity of dollars (and gold) is now produced in 50 percent of the labor time that was socially necessary in former times.[4] The value of paper money in gold and its value in purchasing power are therefore not necessarily identical. They can evolve in opposite directions.

The gold exchange standard, balance of payments, and economic crises

What is characteristic of every system based on the gold standard — whether it is a purely metallic system or a paper money system tied to gold — is *the requirement of adjusting the monetary total to the metallic total, to the "exchange reserves."* If the legal gold cover for the dollar is 25 percent and the exchange reserves do not exceed 25 percent of the total bank notes, every reduction in these reserves leads to a contraction of the monetary total. In effect, it implies a decrease in the quantity of bank notes in circulation. As for credit money, it is ultimately dependent on the amount of bank notes. The whole monetary system becomes an inverted pyramid which is automatically reduced as soon as its base — the gold resting in the vaults of the central bank — contracts.

Experience has shown the capitalists and their economists that a relationship does exist between the total currency in circulation and the rhythm of concentration in general economic activity. The relationship is not a causal one, as many bourgeois schools of political economy incorrectly assume. Every expansion of economic activity is necessarily accompanied by an expansion of monetary income (both wages and profits) under capitalism. Every contraction of economic activity (recession or more serious crisis) leads to a deflation of monetary income (total or partial unemployment reduces the monetary total; profits decline, etc.). If, independently of the economic cycle, the state puts supplementary means of payment into circulation (by increasing unemployment insurance, credits and

subsidies to industry, state purchases, etc.), then the effect of
the recession or crisis is attenuated. However, if, independently
of the economic cycle, the state *reinforces* the deflation through
monetary means (by reducing salaries of public employees,
unemployment insurance and credit to capitalists), then obviously the effect on the recession or crisis is aggravated.

In the first case, total buying power declines less than employment and industrial production; in the second case, total
buying power declines more than employment and production.
One of the reasons the crisis of 1929-32 was so violent was
that, in several key capitalist countries (particularly the United
States, Great Britain, and Germany), a governmental policy
of deflation coincided with a drop in production and employment, which already existed.

However, in a system of paper money tied to the gold standard, the central banks and capitalist governments are compelled to restrict currency circulation as soon as their exchange
reserves decline. All that is needed, then, is that the onset of
a recession coincide with a serious deficit in the balance of
payments, compelling a government to apply a policy of deflation, for an extremely grave economic crisis to erupt. If
the imperialist governments had followed Rueff's advice and
returned to the gold standard, the massive flight of exchange
reserves from France in May-June would have *imposed* a
policy of deflation on the French government as early as that
day, independently of the rise in wages and costs. France
would have quickly experienced tens of thousands of bank-
ruptcies and over a million unemployed.

It was mainly the experience of the 1929-32 crisis and the
fear of a recurrence of such a cataclysm that motivated the
representatives of most of the capitalist countries to go over
to the "gold exchange standard" system at Bretton Woods in
1944. *In this system, the automatic adjustment of the monetary
total to gold reserves* — and consequently, the automatic varia-
tion of total liquid purchasing power to variations in gold
reserves — *is eliminated*. As a matter of fact, in the new system
the exchange reserve of each central bank no longer consists
of gold alone; it includes gold and a certain number of favored
currencies, particularly the dollar and pound sterling. A com-
plicated mechanism, guaranteed by the International Monetary
Fund, operates so that when the gold reserves of a country
decrease, this can be compensated for by "reserve moneys"
(dollars and pounds), or by international credits, or a combination of both. Within each national imperialist economy,
the system is completed through control of the monetary total

by the central bank by means of various instruments: manipulation of discount and interest rates; control of bank credit (one of the principal sources of the creation of money in the capitalist system) through regulating the ratio of liquid assets to current liabilities, etc.

Losses of gold — balance of payments deficits — can result mainly from two movements, at least so far as the imperialist countries are concerned. They can result from an unfavorable trade balance when the deficit is not made up by "invisible" income (interest and dividends on capital invested abroad; international maritime and aviation revenue; income from tourists, etc.). They can result from an export of capital which exceeds a *surplus* in the balance of trade. The first case is true of Great Britain, the second of the United States. The first case indicates that the imperialist country is "living beyond its means," that it is liquidating its reserves. The second indicates that the imperialist country is attempting, on the contrary, to transform — in a disproportionate way — its current revenues and resources currently being produced into long-term investments.[5]

When a country is afflicted with an unfavorable balance of payments, it must liquidate its reserves and go increasingly into debt, all the more multiplying its problems. When the imperialist countries which supply the reserve funds, themselves face a chronic unfavorable balance of payments and settle their deficit by means of their own currency, two reactions in other countries are possible. These latter may need dollars and pounds for trade or military purposes, or may simply find it impossible to refuse this influx of exchange reserves of a particular kind;[6] in this event, the system will function without too much trouble. That was the case with the pound prior to Suez and with the dollar between the Suez crisis and 1964-65. Here the role of money as *means of exchange* (on the political level as well) outweighs its role as *means of payment.*

But if the imperialist countries believe that the influx of exchange reserves is symptomatic of the *inflation* reigning in the United States; that exchange currencies are losing their standing and are constantly losing a part of their purchasing power; that the accumulation of dollar exchange reserves will result in the long run in a substantial loss in the value of their reserves,[7] because its depreciation makes a devaluation of the dollar in terms of gold inevitable — then they will seek to convert increasing amounts of dollars which they hold as exchange reserves into gold, and the whole monetary system will be plunged into crisis. In this case, the role of reserve money as a *means of payment* and as a *stockpile of value* (reserve) overshadows its role as a *means of exchange*.

Countries whose currencies are not reserve currencies must settle deficits in their balance of payment in gold or in dollars; consequently the total of "international liquidities" stays the same. But the United States can settle its balance of payments deficits in dollars. The influx of these dollars into the other imperialist countries immediately widens the base of the inverted pyramid (exactly the same way as an influx of gold in a gold standard system would). Consequently, dollar inflation increases monetary circulation in all the imperialist countries; it feeds and amplifies universal inflation.

But we can never forget that in the final analysis the cause of this inflation is the combination of neocapitalist techniques aimed at avoiding a catastrophic crisis like the one in 1929-32. The cause of dollar inflation is the armament and war policy, the credit bubble in the private sector, growing state, business and private indebtedness.[8] But, catastrophic economic crisis in the United States would automatically spread to all the imperialist countries, so that "choking off" American inflation at any cost would be a remedy worse than the disease for these countries. That is why it can be predicted with certainty that the inflation will persist. The whole debate relates exclusively to its extent and how its costs are to be distributed among the various powers.

There is consequently an inextricable contradiction between the dollar as a weapon of struggle against a crisis in the United States and the capitalist world, on one hand, and as a reserve money in the international monetary system, on the other hand. This contradiction is intensified by a second contradiction, that between the dollar as an international means of exchange and as an international means of payment. In the first role, the dollar should be as abundant as possible, which means in practice that its supply should be "flexible" and its value, consequently, unstable. In its second role, the dollar should be as stable as possible, which means that its supply should rigidly conform to needs, since every oversupply of token money automatically undermines its value.

This contradiction reflects a conflict of interests within the world bourgeoisie. Those who buy and sell products to the United States, the principal sector of the world market, are interested in an abundant, even inflationary, supply of dollars; fluctuations in its purchasing power (except for short-term fluctuations) are of little concern to them. But those who hold dollar credits, public and private bonds, large bank deposits, large insurance policies, are obviously interested in maximum stability of the dollar's purchasing power. The central banks on a world scale and most private banks are in the second category; a good number of industrial trusts are in the first (especially if they are heavily indebted in dollars!).

International capital movements

When a balance of payments deficit is the result of an unfavorable trade balance, there can hardly be any question about the causes for losses in exchange reserves. We should note in passing, however, that such a balance of trade deficit does not necessarily reflect a basic weakness in a capitalist economy. In the nineteenth century, British capitalism could permit itself the luxury of unfavorable trade balances for long periods; its exports of industrial products were chronically lower than its imports of foodstuffs and raw materials. But this deficit was more than compensated for by "invisible" returns, above all from the profits of British foreign investments.

The sudden appearance of balance of payments deficits in countries which do not have chronic trade deficits can have various causes:

a) It can result from a sudden inflation that outstrips the inflation rate of its major imperialist trading partners. There is a sudden deficit in the trade balance, causing a deficit in the balance of payments. This was the case in Italy in 1963 and Japan in 1963-64.

b) It can result from "invisible" expenses which cause chronic deficits. This is one of the causes of the chronic deficits of the United States. Among such "invisible" expenses, the foreign military spending of this imperialist power must be mentioned first.

c) It can result from a chronic excess of capital exports relative to a still favorable balance of trade, but not sufficiently favorable to finance such exports. This is in part the present situation of the United States.[9]

d) It can result from a sudden movement of short-term capital.

In the fourth category, we must distinguish between two types of capital movement. The first reflects the general phenomenon of "overcapitalization" of the imperialist countries, the existence of several billions of dollars which are not invested on a long-term basis, which are looking for quick gains, and which are quickly transferred from one country to the next on the basis of two criteria: the going interest rate, and forecasts of fluctuations in the purchasing power (the "value") of various national currencies. "Hot money" movements in and out of London have been widely cited to explain the numerous "squalls" that have hit the pound since the end of the second world war.

The second type of capital movement is linked to the appearance of big multinational trusts, the *multinational corporation*. Since, by definition, it has ramifications in a great many countries and its dimensions are gigantic (the annual transactions may well pass the state budget of a capitalist nation of average importance), it may have reasons for single transfers involving tens of millions of dollars from one country to another. Such capital movements can provoke important fluctuations in foreign exchange rates, which oscillate around official exchange rates in accordance with the law of supply and demand. Moreover, these world trusts possess important reserves of liquid funds and are consequently interested in the rapid transfer of these reserves from one country to another when the slightest threat of monetary depreciation appears on the horizon. Even a fluctuation in exchange rates on the order of 2 percent can represent a gain or loss of half a million dollars to a firm having liquid reserves of $25 million distributed in five important countries. Clearly the first type of capital movement— "speculation"— and the second type, which is directly connected with the international concentration of capital, are not entirely different from each other but have a tendency to be interdependent. 10

Further these two types of capital movement cannot be considered as being independent of the fundamental situation in each of the imperialist powers and of the capitalist system as a whole. In the final analysis, what takes place in the sphere of circulation reflects what is happening in the sphere of production. The "mistrust" the "speculators" have in a currency expresses their judgment—usually with some foundation—on the future evolution of the balance of payments, that is, on the future solidity of a given currency. Foreseeing the depreciation of a given currency, large holders get rid of it, possibly precipitating its collapse, or at least undermining it in foreign exchange markets. Anticipation of the movement of currencies, accelerates it. But in the last analysis it is not the anticipation that causes the collapse but the movement itself.

This was perfectly illustrated by the recent speculation around the French franc and the German mark. While the sudden movement of capital (surpassing in volume the equivalent of $3 billion between Paris and Zurich and between Paris and

Frankfurt, alone) *precipitated* the monetary crisis of November 1968, it was not at all the *cause* of the crisis; its causes are far deeper.

Since May 1968, the competitive position of French industry has seriously deteriorated because of increased wage costs as well as more rapid inflation. This made a sharp deficit in the balance of trade inevitable, and that is the real source of the "mistrust," along with the bad humor of the big capitalists at the increase in estate duties and certain taxes affecting the bourgeoisie (which the bourgeois press, with its sublime sense of the appropriate, characterized after the event as "clumsy").

In contrast, the West German economy finds itself in a triply favorable situation following the 1966-67 recession. Prices are relatively stable, with its competitive position improving not only in respect to "natural" competitors like Great Britain, Japan, France, and Italy, but even in respect to the United States (from June 1965 to June 1968, the consumer price index increased 7 points in West Germany, 9 points in Italy, 10 points in the U. S., 12 points in France, and 14 points in Great Britain). The growth rate of the total currency, from 1962 to the end of 1967, remained only 5 percent above the growth rate of the gross national product in West Germany, whereas in France the difference rose to 15 percent. Military and unproductive charges weighing down the budget are lighter in West Germany than in any other imperialist power, so that the internal mechanism of automatic inflation works more moderately there than elsewhere. Finally, the mark is not a reserve currency and will not become one, so that it is more sheltered from speculation on its future movement than other foreign exchange. That is the real reason why capital, which turned away from the French franc and the pound sterling, moved toward Germany.

Moreover, it can be stated that in the last analysis — without giving this formula a mechanical meaning — the relationship of forces in the foreign exchange of the imperialist countries (the average and long-term fluctuations of their currency exchange rates) reflects the relationship of real economic strength, the different levels of their productivity, their competitive capacity on the world market. The weakening of the dollar, whatever its contradictory aspects, and we will come back to these, is a fair reflection of a relative decline in the power of U. S. imperialism within the world capitalist system, above all compared to its close competitors (and allies).

Reforms of the international monetary system

The world bourgeoisie is obviously not passive in face of

the constant deterioration of its international monetary system. Over the years, one reform project after another has been tried. Various projects have been discussed at semigovernmental levels, a particularly noteworthy occasion being the last annual meeting of the International Monetary Fund in September-October in Washington (on the eve of the November 1968 squall, which, let us note in passing, was not foreseen at all). An analysis of these various reform projects will permit us to get a closer look at the contradictions afflicting the whole international capitalist economy as well as its interimperialist contradictions.

1) *Return to the gold standard.* This is the thesis propounded by Jacques Rueff in France and supported by the Gaullist regime. We have already indicated its dangers, which big capital and its economists are fully aware of. There is no chance whatever that this reform would be acceptable to the international bourgeoisie, beginning with the Anglo-American capitalists. De Gaulle displays the mentality of a conservative petty stockholder in his blind confidence in the "metal of unchanging value." It is the voice of his peasant ancestors, stuffing gold coins in woolen socks in the process of primitive accumulation.

It has been more than a century since the industrial capitalists, as opposed to usurers and rentiers, found out, in Marx's terms, that the quantity of social labor serving to produce the metallic means of exchange and payment represents nothing more than an overhead cost in social production, consequently reducing the real productive forces. It is in the interest of the system to reduce this quantity rather than increase it. [11]

2) *The revaluation of gold.* In the spirit of Rueff's proposition, a return to the gold standard would have to be accompanied by an increase in the price of gold, possibly to double its present price (from \$35 to \$70 an ounce). On one hand, this would stimulate gold production and cause it to flow into the vaults of the central banks. [12] On the other hand, it would allow these banks to eliminate the use of reserve money since the entire present monetary circulation of the imperialist powers, and even a new expansion of these means of circulation, could rest on the present mass of gold, substantially revaluated. Clearly this solution, without the accompaniment of a return to the gold standard, is highly tempting to the imperialist powers. Undoubtedly it is the road being taken, in stages. Establishment of the two-price system for gold (one price on the private free market and one paid by central banks), in March 1968, marks a step toward abandoning the price of \$35 an ounce established in 1934.

What would such a reform mean? It would simply express

the general inflation, without in the slightest degree eliminating the basic forces and causes and without even masking them. For thirty years, we are told, all prices have risen (in paper money) while the price of gold has remained stable. They forget rather quickly that in the same period there has been a prodigious upsurge in labor productivity in virtually every industrial branch, while nothing equivalent to this has happened in the gold industry.[13] Expressed as values, that is, as quantities of labor socially necessary to produce both categories, the relationship between gold and other goods has therefore developed strongly in the direction of a *drop in value* for goods, as expressed in terms of gold.

By revaluating the "price of gold," we would undoubtedly wind up with a closer view of the relative relationships between the value of gold and that of other goods. But the end result would be to "legalize the rise in prices, after a fashion, and even to stimulate this rise. (There is hardly any doubt that a rise in the price of gold would launch a process of general increase in the monetary total.) *The decline in the value of commodities*— relative to that of gold— *would therefore be expressed in a sharp increase in their price*. There is no better way of saying that the means of exchange— paper money— is being greatly inflated.

Let us add, also, that while gold is obviously undervalued under present circumstances, no one can authoritatively state what the normal market price of the metal would be if there were no official price set by the central banks. The present prices on the free market are heavily tainted by speculation in anticipation of a raise in the price of gold by the central banks. A real comparison of its value— a calculation of the quantity of labor, at worldwide average productivity, necessary to produce an ounce of gold— could provoke quite a few surprises.[14]

3) *Devaluation of the dollar.* Increasing the "price of gold" would really signify a general devaluation of all currencies attached to the same gold exchange standard. But if such a devaluation occurred, the reciprocal relationships between the imperialist currencies might be reviewed. For instance, it might be the occasion for U. S. imperialism to put through a devaluation of the dollar, particularly in relation to certain currencies like the mark, the Swiss franc, the florin, even the yen and the lira. The industrial section of the American bourgeoisie could in this way reduce the enormous spread in wage costs relative to those of its immediate competitors. This would arrest the disquieting rise of imports on the American market,

and at the same time stimulate American exports. In reciprocity, the competitors of American imperialism are obviously reluctant to do this. Reluctance shifts to indignation when projects of this kind are suggested to those bourgeois — bankers or rentiers — who possess large holdings of obligations payable in dollars.

4) *The unification of the Common Market currencies and their use as reserve money.* The creation of a "Eurofranc" has been under study for a long time. If it is to become a reality, more than unification of exchange reserves on a European scale is necessary; the establishment of a European state power is also required. Both are inconceivable in the absence of a far more advanced stage of European interpenetration of capital. For European capitalists to surrender the idea of "national sovereignty" and the use of the national state as an instrument in the defense and guarantee of monopoly profits, it is essential that their interests, the property of these monopolies, should first be Europeanized. On the occasion of the devaluation of the pound, the possibility was brought up of a fusion between the pound and this "Eurofranc." The new currency would take over the functions of reserve money which the pound is fulfilling in an increasingly unsatisfactory way. This obviously presupposes the entry of Great Britain into the Common Market and the participation of the British bourgeoisie in the creation of great European monopolies to confront their American competitors. But even if these conditions were fulfilled, and if the Eurofranc, as a consequence of the preponderant position Western Europe would again occupy on the world market,[15] could really fill the role of reserve currency for small imperialist countries (such as the Scandinavian countries, Australia, New Zealand) and for semicolonial countries particularly, this would only mark a return to the situation at the beginning of the 1950s, which would wind up with the same result after a certain period. For the Eurofranc would be implacably subjected to inflation, unless the European capitalists would prefer a crash of the depth of 1929. And inflation of the reserve currency would trigger the mechanism of a crisis in the international monetary system.

5) *The creation of a world paper money, "central bank money."* The crisis in the gold exchange standard system stems from the unavoidable inflation which attacks currency reserves, *by virtue of their function as countercyclical instruments* within the imperialist nations which issue them (and when we say "countercyclical," we obviously also imply "instruments of permanent war spending," etc.). To avoid this congenital flaw, some economists have thought up a very simple solution:

Why not create a reserve money which would *have no circulation* in any national economy at all but would only be a
"central bank currency"?

This money would stand outside national inflationary pressures. It would be administered by a world council of central
bank governors (or ministers of finance), who would exercise
strict discipline. Its issuance would depend exclusively on the
requirements of world trade and not upon the particular needs
of some national power. It would be "as good as gold," because
of its issue in strictly limited and measured quantities. It would
solve the problem of scarcity in international liquidities and
would avoid all the crises of the present system. In other words,
it is a project to create a "world money." And the famous "special drawing rights" thought up last March are a first step,
a rather modest one it is true, along this road.

The first important proposal along these lines was made
by Keynes in 1943; he had even found a name for this world
money, *"the bancor."* At Bretton Woods, the British again advanced the proposal, which was then forgotten until the crisis
in the international monetary system brought it up again twenty
years later.

These proposals run into two insurmountable difficulties. In
the first place, it is not true that such a system would be freed
from the inflation of various "national" currencies. In reality,
if the balance of payments of a country is unfavorable, and if
it rejects deflation as the means for avoiding economic crisis,
it will wind up by losing all of its gold, if it does not secure
a supplementary quantity of "world reserve money." Universal
inflation would wind up driving gold out of the exchange
reserves of the principal debtor countries. Their reserves would
begin to consist more and more exclusively of "world money";
the quantity of this money issued would in turn increase in
a greater proportion than world exchanges, under the threat
of forcing imperialist countries into deflation which they would
certainly reject. The inflation of "natio₁al" currencies would
therefore have repercussions on the "world money".

Also, such a "world money," administered by a "world council," presupposes a group of experts "independent" of every
government and every specific imperialist power, which is a
fiction, or presupposes a total and unfailing solidarity among
the imperialist powers, which is a fantasy. Unquestionably
a certain *degree* of solidarity exists among the powers in face
of a "common danger" (not only the bureaucratized workers'
states, or the socialist revolution, as in May 1968 in France,
but also the danger of a crash of the whole international mon-

etary system). The real situation, however, is more complex; it is a *dialectical unity of solidarity and of competition among imperialist powers*. So long as there are divergent interests and competition, the "neutrality" of an "administrative council" is completely illusory; it could only reflect the relationship of forces among powers, a relationship, moreover, which is always in flux. An "administrative council of world money above the fray" (the fray of interimperialist conflicts being meant here, not the conflicts between antagonistic social forces) really presupposes a "world government," that is, "super-imperialism," a fusion of imperialist interests through co-ownership of the principal monopolies on a world scale. We are far from that state of affairs.

The conclusion is clear: *all* of the applicable reforms of the world monetary system represent nothing but extensions of international inflation. The latter can really be suppressed only at the price of a return to the orthodox gold standard, at the price of a new economic crisis of extreme gravity. The reforms are directed at best toward attenuating the crisis in the international monetary system, not to eliminating it. This crisis will endure as long as the capitalist mode of production still manages to survive.

Significance of the international monetary crisis

On the historic scale, development of the productive forces is increasingly rebelling not only against private property in the means of production but also against the narrow limits of the national state, in which this development is being increasingly stifled. Like interimperialist wars — virtually impossible today because of the threats hanging over the whole system — the attempt at economic integration of capitalist Europe, the propaganda for the "Atlantic community," the appearance of institutions such as the "Group of Ten" (which unites the major imperialist powers), or the "gold pool," agitation favoring a world money — all of these represent the efforts of the imperialist bourgeoisie to resolve these contradictions in its own way. At the same time, they reflect the impossibility of reaching stable results along this road.

The world is ripe for economic planning on a global scale. This implies a single world money, which can eliminate in a major way the overhead cost involved in the production of gold for monetary ends. But only socialism is capable of realizing these possibilities and the promises they contain. For capitalism, they will remain an eternal mirage. One cannot plan world money on a global scale, that is, the sphere of circulation, without simultaneously planning production. The combination of a "controlled money" and anarchy in production has wound up in a permanent inflation in each imperialist nation. It is hard to see why it would wind up differently on the international level.

Private property in the means of production, meaning decentralization of important investment decisions, implies the inevitability of economic swings and anarchy in production. The irreducible spread between the increase in the capacity of social production implicit in capitalism and the limits it imposes on the capacity for consumption by the masses, gives these fluctuations and this anarchy its periodic crises of overproduction. Neocapitalism, the third stage in the development of capitalism, cannot evade these fluctuations and these crises any more than could free competitive capitalism or classical imperialism. It can only amortize the most serious crises into more moderate recessions, at the cost of permanent inflation.

While inflation—so long as it remains moderate—is not incompatible with a more or less normal functioning of monopoly capitalism in the principal imperialist countries, it contains the danger of increasingly disturbing the world exchanges as soon as it provokes a serious crisis in the international monetary system through the inflation of international reserve currencies. This is the stage now making its debut in the history of neocapitalism. The imperialist powers will search for and apply partial remedies. Each of the remedies will reflect, apart from any desire to reform the system itself, the special competitive interests existing at each specific stage. Inflation itself will not be throttled.

The privileged position that the dollar occupied in the international monetary system for two decades reflected the exceptional situation of the American economy and the power of American imperialism within the international capitalist system. This situation has gradually changed; this power is in relative decline. Every reform of the international monetary system, however unviable it may be, will therefore necessarily reflect the new relationship of forces within the system; it will greatly reduce or even eliminate the role of the pound, reduce the role of the dollar, and will also reduce the role of gold. These relationships of forces will finally settle the question whether it will be a unified European foreign exchange or partial experiments with "world money" which will be substituted for the declining roles of gold, the pound and even the dollar, in their character as international means of payment.[16]

Every adjustment of the international monetary system, as

well as every change in national monetary parities, is not only a weapon in interimperialist competition; it is also an instrument in the national and international class struggle. Big capital always concentrates its efforts on getting the workers to bear the expenses of monetary inflation and of its "reform." The crisis of the international monetary system therefore *tends to sharpen class conflicts within the imperialist countries,* since it reflects an exacerbation of interimperialist competition — with each bourgeois class attempting to "put its own house in order," that is, improve its own competitive position at the expense of its own workers. Manifestations of this trend have multiplied in Europe during the past four or five years; they will soon cross the Atlantic to hit the United States and Canada, then Japan.

The question whether in the long run all the artifices that keep the colossal inverted pyramid of credits, debts, and inflated paper money standing will cave in, and whether recessions will wind up in a new crash like 1929, is not of major interest to the revolutionary movement at this stage. Marxism never tied the perspective of socialist revolution to one of an economic crisis of exceptional gravity such as the 1929 crisis (truly unique in the entire history of capital). It has simply related this perspective to the economic and social contradictions of the system. These contradictions, including the impossibility of avoiding economic crises and fluctuations, are visible and palpable today as they were yesterday, even if the crises are less serious than that of 1929 or 1937 (recessions are just that — less serious crises than those two, particularly in the number of unemployed they create).

By intensifying social conflicts, the international monetary crisis reveals the sickness of the whole system. At the same time, it creates increasingly favorable situations for class struggles opening up prerevolutionary periods, such as those which France experienced in May-June 1968. [17] It is up to revolutionaries to utilize these contradictions, struggles, and recessions in order to bring about the overthrow of capitalism, which is objectively possible. To spout about a "great crash like 1929" too often covers a refusal to understand the possibilities already existing and a refusal to take advantage of them.

December 1, 1968

Notes

[pages 5-31]

Introduction

1. At the end of 1960, "short-term liabilities to foreigners" (dollars held abroad) amounted to $18.7 billion. The U. S. gold stock was $17.8 billion. (*Statistical Abstract of the U. S.*, 1971, p. 756.)

2. Tome II, p.34 (Paris: Julliard, 1962). In English, *Marxist Economic Theory* (New York: Monthly Review Press, 1968), Vol. II, p. 532.

3. *Statistical Abstract of the U. S.*, 1971, pp. 753 and 755.

4. *Monthly Labor Review* (a U. S. government publication), August 1971, p. 5.

5. *Stastical Abstract of the U. S.*, 1966, p. 845.

6. Ibid., 1971, p. 756.

7. ". . . the growing American involvement in Vietnam brought heavy United States pressure on the British to build up their defense of Malaysia and Singapore, the other half of an Anglo-American nutshell in which [John Foster] Dulles' successors planned to contain Asian communism. Malaysia's confrontation with Sukarno in the early 1960s was the last straw for sterling. What was supposedly an era of retreat from Empire, and of subsidence in the cold war, saw a major build-up of Britain's overseas bases and a doubling of the number of servicemen abroad." (Brian Johnson, *The Politics of Money* [New York: McGraw-Hill, 1970], pp. 235-6.)

8. *Monthly Labor Review*, August 1971, p. 5.

9. Ibid.

10. Ibid.

11. *Statistical Abstract*, 1966, p. 845.

12. *New York Times*, May 27, 1972.

13. "The Monetary Crisis Continues," p. 94.

14. Ibid.

Part I

1. Ramsay MacDonald (1866-1937) became prime minister in the first British Labour government in 1924. He bolted the Labour Party in 1931 during his second term as prime minister to form a "national unity" cabinet with the Conservative Party.

2. Frank Cousins, general secretary of the Transport and General Workers Union.

3. Heinrich Bruening (1885-1970) was the leader of the Catholic Center Party. He was appointed German chancellor by Hindenburg in March 1930. He ruled by decree from July 1930 until his dismissal in May 1932.

4. The German title is *Die EWG und die Konkurrenz Europa-Amerika — The Common Market and European-American Competition* (Frankfurt: Europaeische Verlagsanstalt, 1968). The English edition was published in the United States by Monthly Review Press, New York, 1970. Chapter Eight of this edition is used here with permission of the publisher. It has been slightly edited to conform more closely to the original German edition.

5. Are American capital exports cause or effect of the country's balance of payments deficit — in other words, of American inflation? To put the question in these terms, as apologists of the Gaullist regime did, is to condemn oneself to misunderstand the mechanisms governing the international movement of capital in the era of multinational corporations. In fact, if American inflation ceased and the balance of payments deficit disappeared, the export of capital would probably be stimulated. Great Britain had a balance of payments surplus for a whole century — from the battle of Waterloo to the pistol shot at Sarajevo — and this did not prevent her from investing £4 billion in gold abroad (Michael Barratt Brown, *After Imperialism*, Hillary House, New York, 1963, p. 75). It was precisely this balance of payments surplus that allowed British capital to finance those investments without inflation. — E. M.

6. Here we must also include the fact that the American net capital export of $2 billion in the first half of 1966 ($2.7 billion in the first half of 1965) contrasts with a net *import* of capital returns in the amount of $2.1 billion in the first half of 1966 ($2.3 billion in the first half of 1965). Just as British capital in its heyday prior to World War I, American capital today can allow itself the luxury of financing its voluminous export of capital with the interest of capital already invested in foreign countries. If the export of capital to Europe decreased, the result would be that the USA would extract more capital from Europe than it invested there. That is, the negative side of the exploitation would be sharpened while the positive would disappear. It is precisely this capital drain on a global scale which formed the chief argument of the opponents of U. S. imperialism in India prior to the first and second world wars and presently in Latin America. — E. M.

7. See, amongst others, Jacques Rueff, *L'age de l'inflation,* Editions Payot, Paris, 1967. — E. M.

8. This partly corresponds to a concerted French attack on the dollar. At the end of March 1967, gold comprised 91.85 percent of the gross reserves of the Banque de France against an average of 78.11 percent for the EEC central banks and 71.43 percent for the Banque de France in 1958. But between 1958 and 1967, the

proportion of gold in the foreign exchange reserves of the Bundesbank also rose, from 46.04 percent to 64 percent, and similar statistics for the Italian central bank are 50.77 to 68 percent. The whole responsibility cannot therefore be laid at the door of French policy. Furthermore the inevitable result of a reduction of American exchange reserves was an increased risk of a dollar devaluation. The West European central banks were forced to defend themselves against this risk by keeping a larger proportion of their total reserves in gold. The increasing danger of a dollar devaluation accentuated the trend towards gold hoarding with the result that in 1966 for the first time none of the gold mined (worth $1.44 billion) found its way into the vaults of the central banks, and their overall stock of gold actually fell by $95 million. Rueff's campaign to raise the price of gold obviously encouraged this private hoarding of gold. — E. M.

9. R. S. Cooke, president of the South African Chamber of Mines, which provides 74 percent of the gold produced in the capitalist world, stated on June 28, 1967, that the production of South African gold mines could slump to a sixth of its present tonnage in a few years, since production costs were continuously rising and gold prices were not. — E. M.

10. *L'Echo de la Bourse* (Brussels), November 15, 1967. It is very difficult to calculate the true world demand for nonmonetary gold if the dollar were turned into a pure paper currency. The demand for commercial and ornamental gold is estimated to be some half a billion dollars a year, about a third of the annual gold production. Debts and bonds in dollars outside the USA are worth about $30 billion of which only a half is privately owned. The value of gold hoarded by individuals in the whole world is estimated to be $20 billion. In recent years, it has been rising at the rate of $1 billion a year, a trend which had accelerated since 1965 — confirmed by the $3.2 billion decrease in the gold stored in the vaults of the central banks. Hoarding has absorbed three years' gold production plus $3.2 billion worth, a total of about $7.5 billion worth of gold. — E. M.

11. In *La monnaie et les systemes monetaires,* by Bertrand Nogaro, published as long ago as 1948 (Eng. tr. *A Short Treatise on Money and Monetary Problems,* Staples Press, London, 1949), there is a vigorous refutation of the dogma of the gold standard. See also Robert Mosse, *Les problemes monetaires internationaux,* Editions Payot, Paris, 1967. — E. M.

12. Net private indebtedness in the United States increased from $140 billion in 1945 to $753 billion in 1963. In 1945 it was equivalent to 78 percent of gross private income and in 1963 to 143 percent (Harry Magdoff, "Problems of United States Capitalism" in *The Socialist Register,* Monthly Review, New York, 1965, p. 68). By 1966 the sum had reached the figure of $965 billion and gross private indebtedness had passed the $1,000 billion mark. — E. M.

13. The attempt at orthodox budgeting led to quasi stagnation of production and incomes in the Eisenhower period. In fixed prices, per capita consumer spending rose from $1,723 per annum in 1955 to $1,847 in 1961, a rise of 1.2 percent a year. There was a recession in 1957-58 and another in 1960-61; in other words the intercycle period shrank to three years. In the first nine months of the

1957-58 recession, industrial production fell 13.1 percent (compared with 15.9 percent in the first nine months of the 1929 world economic crisis). The United States was only saved from a second 1929 disaster by an inflationary monetary policy and by immense public, especially military, expenditure (see *Economic Report of the President,* together with the *Annual Report of the Council of Economic Affairs,* U.S. Government Printing Office, Washington, January 1962; and Geoffrey Moore, "Measuring Recession," in *The Journal of the American Statistical Society,* June 1958). — E. M.

14. The events of May 1968 and the financial crisis of November that year demonstrated the extreme vulnerability of France's capit-st economy. In four days France lost a quarter of her reserves id on two occasions the franc was only saved by the massive sup-rt of the central banks (especially that of the USA). — E. M.

15. Eurodollars (about $20 billion at the beginning of 1968) are ollars held by central banks in both East and West Europe and by ivate industry and individuals, and deposited by them in private uropean banks. These banks either lend them to other central banks : to American banks or companies. The Eurodollar system has a ro-fold origin. There are higher returns on Eurodollars than on ollar deposits in banks in the USA, and Eurodollars can still be borrowed when the sources of credit in the USA are exhausted. Thus the Eurodollar system has created an international money market which has widened the channels of credit but which has also given impetus to the inflation of international credit and the instability of the international monetary system. It reflects a certain abundance of European capital available for short-term loans to the American capitalist system which can invest it for long-term profits (see Paul Einzig, *The Eurodollar System,* St. Martin's, New York, 1967, and the Thirty-Eighth Annual Report of the Bank of International Settlements, Basle, 1968). — E. M.

16. R. Mosse, op. cit., p. 147. — E. M.

17. *La Libre Belgique,* 19/20 March 1968. — E. M.

18. *The Economist* (November 26, 1966) detailed the relationship between the central banks' tight credit policy and the present recession. The theory of crises explains how an overall shortage in the capital market can go hand-in-hand with increased liquidity on the money market (typified by high interest rates). This liquidity is to some extent the result of the existence of Eurodollars (see *L'Echo de la Bourse* (Brussels), June 28, 1967). — E. M.

19. Michael Barratt Brown, *Labour and Sterling,* The Institute of Workers' Control, Pamphlet Series, No. 3, Nottingham, 1968. — E. M.

20. Robert Triffin, *The World Money Maze,* Yale University Press, New Haven, 1966. — E. M.

21. Karl Schiller, the West German economics minister.

22. A French expression meaning to work for little or nothing. The early kings of Prussia were notorious for penny-pinching.

23. The agreements with the unions which ended the May-June general strike.

24. The French daily, equivalent in standing to the *New York Times* or the London *Times.*

25. The second round of wage negotiations provided for in the

Grenelle agreements of May 1968.

26. This refers to the election of Social Democrat Willy Brandt as chancellor of West Germany by the Bundestag on October 21, 1969.

27. The strike wave referred to involved nearly a million workers in the metals and related industries who walked off their jobs in a series of wildcat strikes beginning September 2, 1969.

28. *Traite d'Economie Marxiste* (Paris: Juliard, 1962), Tome II, page 34. In English, *Marxist Economic Theory* (New York: Monthly Review Press, 1968), Vol. II, p. 532.

29. See "The Crisis of the International Monetary System" in Part II of this book, p. 114.

30. These figures understate the reality because they take into account the partially unemployed only in Italy, Japan, and France, and not in the USA, Great Britain, and Canada. Nor do they include the millions of people who, as the bourgeois economists put it so elegantly, "have withdrawn from the labor market" because they were convinced that they could not find a job. — E. M.

31. Sections I and II of this editorial begin on p. 79 of this book.

32. "To the city (Rome) and to the world." The words with which the pope formerly accompanied benedictions pronounced on the Catholic world during certain solemn church festivals.

33. This refers to the decision of the French government, announced August 23, 1971, to maintain the pre-August 15 fixed exchange rate for the 75 percent of transactions concerned with trade but allow the franc to float for capital and tourist transactions.

Part II

1. See Karl Marx, *Capital*, Vol. II, Part I, Chapter 6, Section 3. In periods of acute economic crisis, when the need for gold shrinks drastically and the precious metal flows out of the market into hoards, this trend is obviously interrupted. At such times, many so-called marginal mines may be closed, as was the case during the 1929-33 crisis. — E. M.

2. "A general fall in prices can result only from a fall in the value of commodities — the value of money [of gold — E. M.] remaining constant. . . . " (Karl Marx, *Capital*, Vol. I, Part I, Chapter 3, Section 1, p. 99, Progress Publishers, Moscow, 1965.) — E. M.

3. Under a gold standard system, gold is the instrument for measuring prices; these are expressed relative to a precise quantity of gold, for example, a pound. Under these conditions, the "price of gold" would be expressed in the following way: 1 gram of gold is worth .002 pounds of gold, which is obviously tautological. Under a paper money system, tied to gold, this would still be true. If by definition $1 equals 1 gram of gold, the expression "the price of gold is $28 an ounce (of 28 grams)" is meaningless; it is not a question of price but the result of a fixed gold coverage of paper money. It is obviously no longer the same thing when bank notes are issued in a larger amount than the total gold held at the central bank. When monetary tokens are involved, their value relative to gold is a measure of their quantity. The "price of gold" under

these conditions would be the reciprocal of the value of the paper money. Under the actual regime of a gold-exchange standard, the "price of gold" represents the value of the dollar in terms of gold, fixed by the Federal Reserve System of the United States. — E. M.

4. We are obviously simplifying. The monetary total does not serve solely as a means of exchange for commodities; it also serves as a means of payment. — E. M.

5. A current deficit in the balance of payments always indicates an inflationary situation. Total circulating buying power in the country is greater than the value of goods and services being offered. The excess buying power attracts supplementary foreign products into such a country. — E. M.

6. We should not forget that following the second world war the imperialist countries did not complain about the inflation of dollars but about their short supply on the world market. The unfavorable balance of payments of the United States — especially created by a flow of dollars to Europe and Asia in the form of "foreign aid" — made it possible to overcome this shortage and increase exchange reserves by a much larger amount than the annual production of gold could possibly have furnished. As for the semicolonial countries, which are tributaries of the imperialist countries experiencing generally even more serious inflation than that of the dollar, their bourgeoisie, even today, considers the dollar as real stuff — not "wallpaper money." — E. M.

7. This mishap occurred to several semicolonial governments in the sphere of influence of British imperialism, particularly several Arab countries which are large oil exporters. When the pound was devalued in November 1967, the value of their accumulated exchange reserves was sharply reduced. — E. M.

8. One must not confuse the sources of monetary inflation with the causes of a rising cost of living; the latter are not reducible to the former. Here the pricing policies of the big monopolies must be taken into consideration (what they call "administered prices" and "pricing investment") whereby the monopolies utilize every increase in wages wrested from them by the workers to increase their profit margins. — E. M.

9. We say "in part" because an important percentage of U. S. capital invested abroad, both in Western Europe and in the semicolonial countries, does not entail any real transfer of capital from the United States, but is financed by capital borrowed in those countries. The "capital account" of the United States is practically in equilibrium: The effective export of capital, causing an actual flow of dollars out of the U. S. is balanced by an equivalent return in interest and dividends on previously invested capital. — E. M.

10. On the question of the international concentration of capital, the multinational corporation and their relationship to the growing instability of the international monetary system, see my small book *Europe vs. America* (New York: Monthly Review Press, 1970). — E. M.

11. "The entire amount of labor power and social means of production expended in the annual production of gold and silver intended as instruments of circulation constitutes a bulky item of the *faux frais* of the capitalist mode of production, of the production

of commodities in general. It is an equivalent abstraction from social utilization of as many additional means of production and consumption as possible, i. e., of real wealth. To the extent that the costs
of this expensive machinery of circulation are decreased, the given
scale of production or the given degree of its extension remaining
constant, the productive power of social labor is *eo ipso* increased.
Hence, so far as the expediences developing with the credit system
have this effect, they increase capitalist wealth directly. . . . " (Karl
Marx, *Capital*, Vol. II, Part II, Chapter 17, Section 2, p. 350, Progress Publishers, Moscow, 1967.) — E. M.

12. The attempt to increase the "price of gold" (devalue the dollar)
has been a strong stimulus for gold hoarding over the past few years.
In 1966 and 1967, the equivalent of the entire production of gold
in the capitalist world wound up in the strong boxes of speculators
rather than in the reserves of central banks. It is interesting to note
that Marx, in the paragraph following the one cited in footnote 11,
indicates that without the development of the credit system and of
monetary tokens (credit money), the capitalist system would have
reached a limit based on the volume of production of the precious
metals. — E. M.

13. It is true that a constant rise in production costs, while the
sale price has remained stable for more than thirty years, has
spurred the capitalists exploiting gold mines to increase the rational-
ization of labor and to close marginal mines, so that the average
productivity of labor in this sector has also increased. — E. M.

14. On several occasions, American imperialist leaders have threatened to "demonetize gold." They believe that if the central banks stop
buying gold and throw their complete stocks on the market, the price
of gold — which would then be purchased for industrial use — would
slump. This would have been a far more realistic proposal in the
period when the United States possessed two-thirds of the world's
gold; it is no accident that they did not make it then. Today there
is no chance at all the capitalist governments (let alone the workers'
states) would accept such a proposal. From now on, any "demonetization" could only be partial, and with the help of the inflation
of paper money, gold would continue to be bought, both by governments and individuals, as a guaranty against periodic devaluations of foreign exchange currencies. — E. M.

15. The capitalist countries of Europe have over 50 percent world
exports to their credit. Even if the internal Common Market exchanges
are eliminated from this figure (and there is no justification whatsoever for such a subtraction), the figure would still be above 40 per
cent. — E. M.

16. We must emphasize that the international capitalist economy
is going through a real "crisis in international liquidity" which is
striking the semicolonial countries even more heavily than the imperialist ones. Prior to 1940, the total amount of exchange reserves
for all countries was more or less equal to the value of annual world
imports. In 1964, these reserves (only 60 percent of which were in
gold) represented merely 43 percent of world imports. — E. M.

17. While students played the role of detonator in the May-June
1968 explosion in France, we must not forget that the detonator
could operate only because the explosive material was present. This

explosive material was made up in a very precise way, apart from the general causes which are products of neocapitalism but do not explain why this explosion took place now and not in 1961 or in 1973. Its constituent elements were the residue of unsatisfied workers' demands resulting from the "stabilization plan" of Giscard d'Estaing, the recession which that provoked in 1964, and its "renewal" in the ordinances of 1967; also, by the rise in unemployment among the youth for a year. These two phenomena are tightly linked to inflation and the attempts to restrain it within the framework of interimperialist competition. In this connection, see Daniel Bensaid and Henri Weber, *May 1968: A General Rehearsal*, Maspero, Paris, 1968, pp. 147-151. — E. M.

Glossary

BALANCE OF PAYMENTS: The difference between the sum of the resources a country has sold to other countries in a given period (commodity exports, sale of services abroad, sale of stocks and bonds, etc.) and the sum of the resources it has acquired from other countries in that period (commodity imports, services purchased abroad, military purchases in other countries, purchases of foreign stocks and bonds, etc.). If the resources sold exceed the resources acquired, the country enjoys a balance of payments surplus. If the resources acquired is the larger sum, the country has a payments deficit, which it must offset by the liquidation of a part of its reserves.

BALANCE OF TRADE: The difference between a country's exports and its imports. The balance is said to be positive or in surplus when exports exceed imports. The converse case is termed a trade deficit.

BANK MONEY: See CREDIT MONEY.

BANK RESERVES: The money banks keep available to meet the demands of depositors.

CAPITAL FLIGHT: The sending of funds abroad by corporations and wealthy individuals in anticipation of devaluation or in response to a social crisis.

CENTRAL BANK: A bank that is banker to both the government and other banks and that manages the national currency and credit policy. Most central banks are state-owned; all operate under government supervision. The Federal Reserve is the U. S. central bank. It is owned by its affiliated banks. See also FEDERAL RESERVE SYSTEM.

CONVERTIBILITY: Under the classic gold standard, this term referred to the free exchange of a currency for gold or silver at a fixed price. Now convertibility applies only to foreign holders of a domestic currency. The dollar became totally inconvertible on August 15, 1971.

CREDIT MONEY, BANK MONEY: Checking account deposits that originate from bank loans, mainly to businesses.

CURRENCY RESERVES: A country's holdings of foreign currencies.

DEFLATION: A decline in the amount of money in circulation relative to the number of economic transactions. This leads either to a decline in the volume of goods and services produced and offered for sale, with an accompanying rise of unemployment, or to a fall in prices, usually the former.

DEVALUE, DEVALUATION: An official reduction in the par value of a currency by a lowering of its gold or dollar equivalency. When a country devalues, the prices of its exports in foreign markets are lowered while imports from other countries are made more expensive. See also REVALUE.

EXCHANGE CONTROLS: Government controls on purchases of foreign currencies, the purpose being to prevent a depletion of the country's gold and foreign currency reserves. Such controls are common in Latin America, for example, where governments strictly limit the amount of dollars businesses and individuals may purchase to pay for imported goods.

EXCHANGE RATES: The ratio at which two currencies are traded. If the ratio is held to an extremely narrow range by government action, the exchange rate is said to be fixed. If the ratio is allowed to fluctuate in accordance with the relative buying power of each currency and other factors, the exchange rate or currency in question is said to be floating.

EXCHANGE RESERVES: See RESERVES.

EUROBONDS: Bonds issued in Europe and denominated in dollars.

EURODOLLARS: Dollars held by central banks in Europe and by private industry and individuals, and deposited by them in private European banks, mainly branches of U. S. banks.

FEDERAL RESERVE SYSTEM: The twelve regional Federal Reserve banks, which together make up the central bank of the U. S., and affiliated banks including all national banks and many state banks and trust companies. The Federal Reserve was established in 1913.

FLOATING EXCHANGE RATES, FLOATING CURRENCY: See EXCHANGE RATES.

FOREIGN EXCHANGE: Foreign currencies.

GOLD EXCHANGE STANDARD: This term originally applied to a situation in which countries tied their currencies not to gold but to another currency that was convertible into gold. India and the Philippines, for example, used the gold exchange standard prior to World War I. Its use was extended in the 1920s as a partial solution to an extremely uneven international distribution of gold. The gold exchange standard, with the dollar as the convertible currency to which all other currencies were tied, was adopted for the international monetary system established by the Bretton Woods conference in July 1944. Since then, the term has been practically synonymous with that system. The gold-dollar exchange system was abandoned on August 15, 1971, when President Nixon ended the convertibility of the dollar into gold.

GOLD POOL: Established in 1961 by the United States, Britain, and six continental European countries. Its purpose was to dampen down speculative transactions in gold, through purchases and sales of the metal by members of the pool. It was disbanded after the establishment of the "two-tier" gold market in March 1968. See *Chronology.*

GOLD STANDARD: The currencies of countries operating under the gold standard are tied to gold by means of a government guarantee to buy and sell gold at a fixed price. Under the classic gold standard, abandoned in 1933, this guarantee applied not only to foreign holders of the currency but to citizens of the country concerned as well. This meant that a strict proportionality between currency in circulation and a country's gold reserve had to be maintained. Thus, under the gold standard, gold outflow due to a balance of payments deficit automatically brought deflation and increased unemployment.

HOT MONEY: Funds of wealthy individuals and multinational corporations not invested on a long-term basis but quickly shifted from one country to another (and from one currency to another) in pursuit of quick gains. The shifts are decided on the basis of interest rate fluctuations or anticipated changes in the exchange rates of various national currencies. These flows, sometimes amounting to billions of dollars a day into or out of a single country, can deplete a country's reserves in a few weeks or even days. Such flows can also result in the central bank of a country with a strong currency being inundated by such a deluge of dollars or other weak currency that it can no longer support the old fixed exchange rate. In either case, a currency crisis is precipitated.

INFLATION: An increase in the volume of money and credit relative to available goods, resulting in a rise in the general price level.

INTERNATIONAL LIQUIDITY: The total international means of payment in existence at any given time.

INTERNATIONAL MONETARY FUND (IMF): Established under the Articles of Agreement drawn up at the Bretton Woods Conference in July 1944. One hundred eighteen countries are members. Its purpose is to provide a pool of national currencies that member countries can draw on during temporary balance of payments crises. The currencies and gold making up this reserve fund are paid in by the member countries on the basis of quotas. Each country's quota reflects its relative economic strength, with the U. S. quota being the largest.

Financial assistance to a member government takes the form of a sale by the Fund of the currencies of other members for an equivalent amount of the buyer's own currency. The amount of foreign exchange a member country can buy is a function of its quota, how serious its balance of payments crisis is, and the policy it adopts to eliminate its payments deficit. Since 1969, the IMF also creates and distributes a form of international money called Special Drawing Rights (SDRs). See below.

LIQUIDITY: The availability of cash or assets readily convertible into cash.

MONETARY TOKENS: Money having a greater face value than intrinsic value. For example, paper currency not backed by gold.

MONEY SUPPLY: The stock of money consisting of coin,

paper currency, and checking account balances that is available for carrying on economic transactions within a country.

RESERVES: A country's holdings of international means of payment (gold, SDRs, and certain favored foreign currencies, particularly the dollar and British pound). A country draws upon its reserves to settle deficits in its economic transactions with other countries.

RESERVE CURRENCY: A currency, such as the dollar or British pound, that other countries hold as part of their reserves.

REVALUE, REVALUATION: An official increase in the par value of a currency through an increase of its gold or dollar equivalency. Import prices are decreased and export prices increased as a result. See also DEVALUE.

SDRs, SPECIAL DRAWING RIGHTS: A form of international credit, often referred to as "paper gold," extended by the International Monetary Fund to member countries. SDRs do not circulate within these countries but are used exclusively by governments and central banks as an international means of payment supplementing their gold and foreign currency holdings.

TRADE BALANCE: See BALANCE OF TRADE.